TAPESTRY

Reflection and Beyond

Expanding Written Communication

TAPESTRY

The **Tapestry** program of language materials is based on the concepts presented in ***The Tapestry Of Language Learning:*** *The Individual in the Communicative Classroom* by Robin C. Scarcella & Rebecca L. Oxford.

❖

Each title in this program focuses on:

❖

Individual learner strategies and instruction

❖

The relatedness of skills

❖

Ongoing self-assessment

❖

Authentic material as input

❖

Theme-based learning linked to task-based instruction

❖

Attention to all aspects of communicative competence

TAPESTRY

REFLECTION AND BEYOND

Exanding Written Communication

Laurie Blass
Meredith Pike-Baky

Heinle & Heinle Publishers
A Division of Wadsworth, Inc.
Boston, Massachusetts, 02116, USA

The publication of *Reflection and Beyond* was directed by the members of the Heinle & Heinle ESL Publishing Team:

David Lee, Editorial Director
Susan Mraz, Marketing Manager
Lisa McLaughlin, Production Editor

Also participating in the publication of this program were:

Publisher: Stanley J. Galek
Editorial Production Manager: Elizabeth Holthaus
Assistant Editor: Kenneth Mattsson
Manufacturing Coordinator: Mary Beth Lynch
Full Service Project Manager/Compositor: Monotype Composition Company
Interior Design: Maureen Lauran
Cover Design: Maureen Lauran

Manufactured in the United States of America.

ISBN: 0-8384-2305-1

Heinle & Heinle Publishers is a division of Wadsworth, Inc.

10 9 8 7 6 5 4

To the ESL community—teachers, students, administrators, scholars, and writers—whose commitment to language learning and international understanding continues to inspire us.

PHOTO CREDITS

Chapter 1: 2, a. Molly Shepard/The Cloud Factory; b. Superstock; c. Lou Jawitz/Image Bank; d. Castenda/Image Bank; e. Joel Gordon; f. Bob Daemmrich.

Chapter 2: 14, a Superstock/4x5; b. Rhoda Sidney/Photo Edit; c. Mary Kate Denny/Photo Edit; d. Lewin/Image Bank; e. M. Stewart/Picture Cube; f. Alan Carey/Image Works.

Chapter 3: 31, Copyright © 1992, Alexandro Galindo/Vintage Contemporaries/Random House. Author Sandra Cisneros, for book, *Woman of Hollering Creek: and Other Stories.*

Chapter 4: 40, Mark Antman/Image Works; Gatewood/Image Works; Image Works.

Chapter 5: 52, a. Custom Medical Stock; b. E. Streichan/Superstock; c. Image Works; d. Antman/ Image Works; e. E. Gebhardt/Superstock; f. Lawfer/ Picture Cube; 53, Daemmrich/Image Works; Comstock; W. Hill/Image Works; Strickler/ Image Works; Custom Medical Stock; Tony Freeman/ Photo Edit; 57, Bill Burkhart/ HarperCollins, © 1992; 61 The Art Institute of Chicago, credit under image. 66 AP/WWP; R. Dreschsler/Fotex/Shooting Star International; AP/WWP; Shooting Star International; A. Archer/ Shooting Star International; Shooting Star International; Shooting Star International; AP/WWP.

Chapter 7: 79, a. McGlynn/Image Works; b. Gardner/Image Works; c. Will & Dani McIntyre/ Photo Researchers, Inc.; d. R. Michael Stuckey/ Comstock; e. Joe Viesti; f. Bob Daemmrich; 79, Bob Daemmrich, Annette Lerner/Superstock; Jack Spratt/Image Works; Photo Edit; Photo Edit; 85, The San Francisco Chronicle.

Chapter 8: 92, a. Shooting Star International; b. Shooting Star International; c. Shooting Star International; d. Universal/Shooting Star International; 97, Shooting Star International.

Chapter 10: 116, a. Washnik Studio/Stock Market; b. Okoniewski/Image Works; c. Topham/ Image Works; d. AP/WWP; e. Beebe/Custom Medical Stock; f. Preuss/Image Works; 122, S. Anderson/Picture Cube.

ILLUSTRATIONS AND MAPS

Susan Jones

5, "Trapped Under A Refrigerator," by Antonio Farré. Reprinted by permission of the author. 19, "Mother's Hands, Mother's Eyes," by Marty Williams. 20, "Coach Keating: A Memoir," by Robert Drechsler. Reprinted by permission of the author. 32, From the *House on Mango Street.* Copyright © 1989 by Sandra Cisneros. Published in the United States by Vintage Books, a division of Random House, Inc., New York and distributed in Canada by Random House of Canada Limited, Toronto. Originally published in somewhat different form by Arte Publico Press in 1984 and revised in 1989. Reprinted by permission of Susan Bergholz Literary Services, New York. 44, "Learning Styles," adapted from *The Tapestry of Language Learning* by Robin C. Scarcella and Rebecca L. Oxford, Heinle and Heinle, Boston, 1992. 57, *A Pilgrim At Tinker Creek* by Annie Dillard. Harper's Magazine Press, New York 1974, pp. 4-50. 71, adapted from "The Song Sent Across the Mekong," by T.C. Huo. *Amerasia Journal*, UCLA, 1991. 85, "A Chinese New Year Celebration," by Joyce Jue. Adapted from "Delicious Symbolism of Chinese New Year." *The San Francisco Chronicle*, Wednesday, February 5, 1992, pp. F1& F3. 97, "'Trek VI' Sets Sail on a New Mission (Movie Review)," by Susan Wloszczyna. *USA TODAY*, Friday, December 6, 1991. 109, "Essential Futuristic Gadgets," by Tim Jackson. Reprinted from the *Economist* in *The San Francisco Chronicle,* Thursday, January 16, 1992. 122, "Saving the Planet," by Dr. Helen Caldicott. Adapted from "Saving the Planet," in *Folio*, April 1992, KPFA Program Guide, pp.1 and 26.

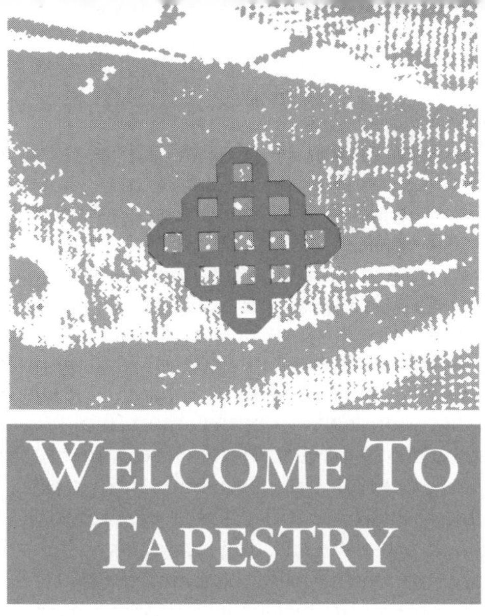

Welcome To Tapestry

Enter the world of Tapestry! Language learning can be seen as an ever-developing tapestry woven with many threads and colors. The elements of the tapestry are related to different language skills such as listening and speaking, reading and writing; the characteristics of the teachers; the desires, needs, and backgrounds of the students; and the general second language development process. When all these elements are working together harmoniously, the result is a colorful, continuously growing tapestry of language competence of which the student and the teacher can be proud.

This volume is part of the Tapestry program for students of English as a second language (ESL) at levels from beginning to "bridge" (which follows the advanced level and prepares students to enter regular postsecondary programs along with native English speakers). Tapestry levels include:

Beginning
Low Intermediate
High Intermediate
Low Advanced
High Advanced
Bridge

Because the Tapestry Program provides a unified theoretical and pedagogical foundation for all its components, you can optimally use all the Tapestry student books in a coordinated fashion as an entire curriculum of materials. (They will be published from 1993 to 1995 with further editions likely thereafter.) Alternatively, you can decide to use just certain Tapestry volumes, depending on your specific needs.

Tapestry is primarily designed for ESL students at postsecondary institutions in North America. Some want to learn ESL for academic or career advancement, others for social and personal reasons. Tapestry builds directly on all these motivations. Tapestry stimulates learners to do their best. It enables learners to use English naturally and to develop fluency as well as accuracy.

Tapestry Principles

The following principles underlie the instruction provided in all of the components of the Tapestry program.

EMPOWERING LEARNERS

Language learners in Tapestry classrooms are active and increasingly responsible for developing their English language skills and related cultural abilities. This self-direction leads to better, more rapid learning. Some cultures virtually train their students to be passive in the classroom, but Tapestry weans them from passivity by providing exceptionally high-interest materials, colorful and motivating activities, personalized self-reflection tasks, peer tutoring and other forms of cooperative learning, and powerful learning strategies to boost self-direction in learning.

The empowerment of learners creates refreshing new roles for teachers, too. The teacher serves as facilitator, co-communicator, diagnostician, guide, and helper. Teachers are set free to be more creative at the same time their students become more autonomous learners.

HELPING STUDENTS IMPROVE THEIR LEARNING STRATEGIES

Learning strategies are the behaviors or steps an individual uses to enhance his or her learning. Examples are taking notes, practicing, finding a conversation partner, analyzing words, using background knowledge, and controlling anxiety. Hundreds of such strategies have been identified. Successful language learners use language learning strategies that are most effective for them given their particular learning style, and they put them together smoothly to fit the needs of a given language task. On the other hand, the learning strategies of less successful learners are a desperate grab-bag of ill-matched techniques.

All learners need to know a wide range of learning strategies. All learners need systematic practice in choosing and applying strategies that are relevant for various learning needs. Tapestry is one of the only ESL programs that overtly weaves a comprehensive set of learning strategies into language activities in all its volumes. These learning strategies are arranged in six broad categories throughout the Tapestry books:

Forming concepts
Personalizing
Remembering new material
Managing your learning
Understanding and using emotions
Overcoming limitations

The most useful strategies are sometimes repeated and flagged with a note, "It Works! Learning Strategy . . ." to remind students to use a learning strategy they have already encountered. This recycling reinforces the value of learning strategies and provides greater practice.

RECOGNIZING AND HANDLING LEARNING STYLES EFFECTIVELY

Learners have different learning styles (for instance, visual, auditory, hands-on; reflective, impulsive; analytic, global; extroverted, introverted; closure-oriented, open). Particularly in an ESL setting, where students come from vastly different cultural backgrounds, learning styles differences abound and can cause "style conflicts."

Unlike most language instruction materials, Tapestry provides exciting activities specifically tailored to the needs of students with a large range of learning styles. You can use any Tapestry volume with the confidence that the activities and materials are intentionally geared for many different styles. Insights from the latest educational and psychological research undergird this style-nourishing variety.

OFFERING AUTHENTIC, MEANINGFUL COMMUNICATION

Students need to encounter language that provides authentic, meaningful communication. They must be involved in real-life communication tasks that cause them to *want* and *need* to read, write, speak, and listen to English. Moreover, the tasks—to be most effective—must be arranged around themes relevant to learners.

Themes like family relationships, survival in the educational system, personal health, friendships in a new country, political changes, and protection of the environment are all valuable to ESL learners. Tapestry focuses on topics like these. In every Tapestry volume, you will see specific content drawn from very broad areas such as home life, science and technology, business, humanities, social sciences, global issues, and multiculturalism. All the themes are real and important, and they are fashioned into language tasks that students enjoy.

At the advanced level, Tapestry also includes special books each focused on a single broad theme. For instance, there are two books on business English, two on English for science and technology, and two on academic communication and study skills.

UNDERSTANDING AND VALUING DIFFERENT CULTURES

Many ESL books and programs focus completely on the "new" culture, that is, the culture which the students are entering. The implicit message is that ESL students should just learn about this target culture, and there is no need to understand their own culture better or to find out about the cultures of their international classmates. This makes some ESL students feel their own culture is not valued in the new country.

Tapestry is designed to provide a clear and understandable entry into North American culture. Nevertheless, the Tapestry Program values *all* the cultures found in the ESL classroom. Tapestry students have constant opportunities to become "culturally fluent" in North American culture while they are learning English, but they also have the chance to think about the cultures of their classmates and even understand their home culture from different perspectives.

INTEGRATING THE LANGUAGE SKILLS

Communication in a language is not restricted to one skill or another. ESL students are typically expected to learn (to a greater or lesser degree) all four language skills: reading, writing, speaking, and listening. They are also expected to develop strong grammatical competence, as well as become socioculturally sensitive and know what to do when they encounter a "language barrier."

Research shows that multi-skill learning is more effective than isolated-skill learning, because related activities in several skills provide reinforcement and refresh the learner's memory. Therefore, Tapestry integrates all the skills. A given Tapestry volume might highlight one skill, such as reading, but all other skills are also included to support and strengthen overall language development.

However, many intensive ESL programs are divided into classes labeled according to one skill (Reading Comprehension Class) or at most two skills (Listening/Speaking Class or Oral Communication Class). The volumes in the Tapestry Program can easily be used to fit this traditional format, because each volume clearly identifies its highlighted or central skill(s).

Grammar is interwoven into all Tapestry volumes. However, there is also a separate reference book for students, *The Tapestry Grammar,* and a Grammar Strand composed of grammar "work-out" books at each of the levels in the Tapestry Program.

Other Features of the Tapestry Program

PILOT SITES

It is not enough to provide volumes full of appealing tasks and beautiful pictures. Users deserve to know that the materials have been pilot-tested. In many ESL series, pilot testing takes place at only a few sites or even just in the classroom of the author. In contrast, Heinle & Heinle Publishers have developed a network of Tapestry Pilot Test Sites throughout North America. At this time, there are approximately 40 such sites, although the number grows weekly. These sites try out the materials and provide suggestions for revisions. They are all actively engaged in making Tapestry the best program possible.

AN OVERALL GUIDEBOOK

To offer coherence to the entire Tapestry Program and especially to offer support for teachers who want to understand the principles and practice of Tapestry, we have written a book entitled, *The Tapestry of Language Learning: The Individual in the Communicative Classroom* (Scarcella and Oxford, published in 1992 by Heinle & Heinle).

A Last Word

We are pleased to welcome you to Tapestry! We use the Tapestry principles every day, and we hope these principles—and all the books in the Tapestry Program—provide you the same strength, confidence, and joy that they give us. We look forward to comments from both teachers and students who use any part of the Tapestry Program.

Rebecca L. Oxford
University of Alabama
Tuscaloosa, Alabama

Robin C. Scarcella
University of California at Irvine
Irvine, California

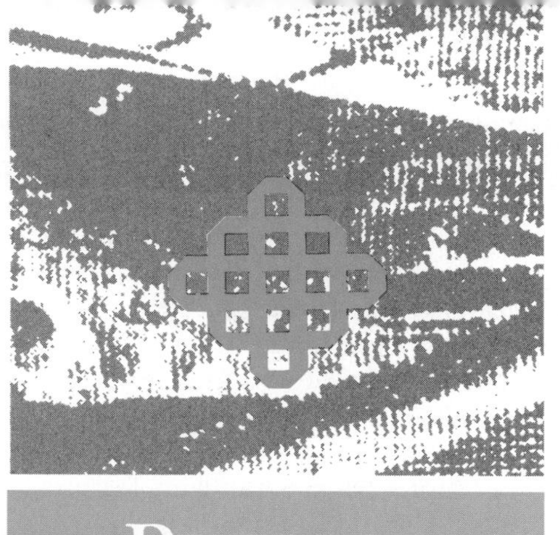

PREFACE

We designed *Reflection and Beyond: Expanding Written Communication* to address the needs of ESL students in low-intermediate academic writing courses. The text, therefore, springs from our contention that students at this level, at the threshold of becoming independent, fluent writers, need to:

- focus on mainly personal writing, but be given a solid introduction to abstract writing
- progress from shorter assignments to longer ones
- practice writing without stringent demands to follow prescriptive models that force them into "cookie-cutter" formats (e.g., the "comparison/contrast essay")
- manipulate the language, writing conventions, and ideas related to a topic before they write about it
- read, discuss, and write about stimulating, timely, and intercultural topics
- choose from a variety of writing assignments, as well as vary the existing ones to suit their needs and interests
- evaluate and revise their work as part of the writing process
- share ideas and concerns with peers through pair, small group, and cooperative activities
- become increasingly independent thinkers and writers

Reflection and Beyond: Expanding Written Communication takes these needs into consideration within the thematic framework of reflection. By reflection, we are implying that writing can be a means to self-discovery. The theme unfolds gradually as students move from writing within the personal realm (e.g. "Memories", *Chapter 1*) to writing about places, people, and things in their immediate environment (e.g., "Celebrations", *Chapter 7*). Finally, students have the opportunity to write about the individual in relation to more remote dimensions, such as the future and the environment (e.g., "Saving the Planet", *Chapter 10*).

Chapter Organization

We have divided the ten-chapter text into three parts. Part I addresses the prewriting stage, where students begin to form ideas on the chapter topic. Part II presents language and ideas necessary for the final writing assignment. Part III contains writing, evaluating, and rewriting assignments. Each chapter begins with an introduction that ties its theme to the umbrella theme of reflection and establishes the goals of the chapter.

Each chapter has the following features:

PART I

The first section in Part I, **Get Started**, presents the general concepts of the chapter visually, and sometimes aurally. Reading, listening, cooperative information-sharing, and discussions help students manipulate or review ideas and language related to the topic. **Interview** follows, in which students query a partner on his or her personal opinions and/or experience with the topic. Part I ends with a **Quickwrite,** a freewriting assignment on a personal aspect of the topic. Students can save this assignment to use later on in the chapter.

PART II

Part II begins with **Language Expansion,** a presentation of vocabulary and grammar points that relate directly to the writing task of the chapter. Vocabulary activities allow students to review and share their knowledge of lexical items. The grammar section presents a grammatical structure that is germane to the chapter topic (for example, modals in *Chapter 10* ["Saving the Planet"]: "People *should* engage in direct action in order to solve environmental problems.") Students review a simple explanation of the point and examples taken from the reading passage that follows, and then do written practice assignments. The next section, **Read, Discuss, and [writing task of the chapter]** consists of an authentic reading passage geared to the students' level. It serves both as a source of further information on the topic and as a model of one possible approach to writing about the topic. Each passage is framed by pre- and post-reading activities. This section concludes with an activity that points out and practices writing conventions modeled by the passage that will help students with their own writing.

PART III

A section entitled **Gather Information and [writing task]** begins Part III. This section consists mainly of activities for organizing and developing the information students are going to incorporate into their assignments. It may also encourage students to do further research if necessary, and help them narrow down a writing topic. A selection of writing assignments follows, including the opportunity to think of an original topic and write about it. Part III concludes with **Assess**, a section that encourages students to reflect on the writing assignment, evaluate it with a partner, rewrite it, and then look ahead to the next chapter.

Acknowledgments

We gratefully acknowledge David Lee, Rebecca Oxford, and Robin Scarcella for their inspiration, ideas, and encouragement along the way. We also thank Ken Mattsson for his support and gentle prodding. We would also like to acknowledge the contributions of Mary Gill, Robert Drechsler, Gaby Kuaupers, Janet Miller, Howard Rachelson, Joan Rouillard, Rosa Vasquez, Ellen White, and Marty Williams.

In addition, we thank the following reviewers whose comments were invaluable during the developmental stages of this project:

Lauren Lee Moulton, English Language Schools, Santa Barbara, CA
Anca Nemoianu, Catholic University of America, Washington, DC
Julia Yobst, University of Miami, FL

We would also like to thank the following instructors and their students for field testing the material in their classes:

Judy Graves, Eurocenters Alexandria, VA
Collette Green, ICPR Junior College, Mayagüez, PR
John Green, University of Puerto Rico, Mayagüez, PR
Barbara Raiden, Spring International Language Center, Littleton, CO

Reading, Neil Anderson, Ohio University
Grammar, Patricia Byrd, Georgia State University
Syllabus, Darlene Larson, New York University
Writing, Sandra McKay, San Francisco State University
Listening/Speaking, Robert Oprandy, Columbia University
Culture, Thomas Scovel, San Francisco State University
Themes & Tasks, Marguerite Ann Snow, California State University, Los Angeles
Assessment, Merrill Swain, Ontario Institute for Studies in Education

CONTENTS

1 Memories 1

PART I
Get Started 2
Interview 4
Quickwrite 5

PART II
Language Expansion 5
Read, Discuss, and Write About a Memory 7

PART III
Gather Information and Write About a Memory 9
Assess 11

2 A Person You Admire 13

PART I
Get Started 14
Interview 15
Quickwrite 16

PART II
Language Expansion 16
Read, Discuss, and Describe a Person You Admire 19

PART III
Gather Information and Describe a Person You Admire 23
Assess 25

3 Names 27

PART I
Get Started 28
Interview 29
Quickwrite 29

PART II
Language Expansion 30
Read, Discuss, and Write About a Name 31

PART III
Gather Information and Write About a Name 35
Assess 37

4 *Learning Styles* 39

PART I

Get Started 40
Interview 42
Quickwrite 42

PART II

Language Expansion 42
Read, Discuss, and Write About Your Learning Style 43

PART III

Gather Information and Write About Your Learning Style 47
Assess 49

5 *Places* 51

PART I

Get Started 52
Interview 54
Quickwrite 54

PART II

Language Expansion 54
Read, Discuss, and Describe a Place 56

PART III

Gather Information and Describe a Place 60
Assess 62

6 *Music as Personal History* 65

PART I

Get Started 66
Interview 68
Quickwrite 68

PART II

Language Expansion 69
Read, Discuss, and Write About Your Associations With a Song 70

PART III

Gather Information and Write About Your Associations With a Song 74
Assess 75

7 *Celebrations* 77

PART I

Get Started 78
Interview 80
Quickwrite 81

PART II

Language Expansion 81
Read, Discuss, and Describe and Explain a Celebration 84

PART III

Gather Information and Describe and Explain a Celebration 88
Assess 90

8 *Favorite Movies* 91

PART I

Get Started 92
Interview 93
Quickwrite 94

PART II

Language Expansion 95
Read, Discuss, and Express Your Opinion 97

PART III

Gather Information and Express Your Opinion 100
Assess 102

9 Future Gadgets 103

PART I

Get Started 104
Interview 105
Quickwrite 106

PART II

Language Expansion 106
Read, Discuss, and Predict Future Technology 107

PART III

Gather Information and Predict Future Technology 112
Assess 114

10 Saving the Planet 115

PART I

Get Started 116
Interview 117
Quickwrite 118

PART II

Language Expansion 118
Read, Discuss, and Propose a Solution 121

PART III

Gather Information and Propose a Solution 126
Assess 128

Appendices

APPENDIX A

Reflections on My Writing 132

APPENDIX B

Word Lists 133

APPENDIX C

Fluency Starters 136

CHAPTER 1

Memories

Unless we remember, we cannot understand.
—Edward M. Forster, English novelist

Personal writing, writing about yourself and your experiences, is the most reflective of all types of writing. It is where most writers begin. Many writers get started by writing regularly about their thoughts, their day-to-day activities, and their problems. Sometimes they take these short pieces of writing and expand them into longer pieces. Sometimes they discover a love of writing and maybe even a talent for it. Writing begins with what is inside you, so in this chapter, you are going to write about one of your memories.

PART I

Get Started

A. TAKE A LOOK

The following snapshots are special moments from the pasts of several student writers. Look at the pictures and describe what is happening.

a.

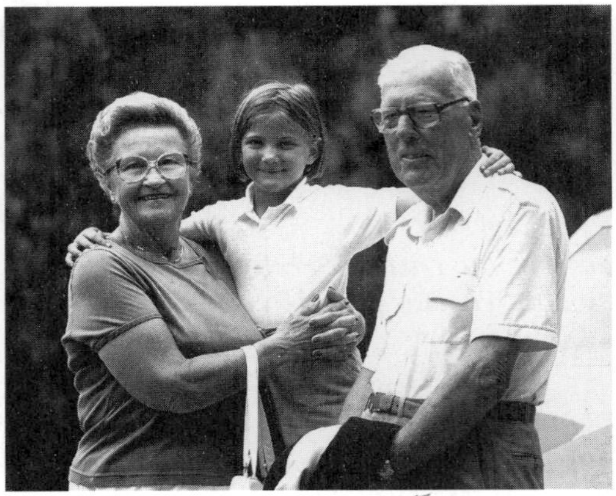

b.

c.

d.

e.

f.

B. LISTEN AND MATCH

Now listen to the students describing their photos. Do this alone. Listen the first time for key words. After you listen a second time, match the descriptions and the photos. Write the number of the description next to the photo it goes with.

C. REMEMBER

Complete the following chart about the memorable moments the students describe in Exercise B. Work with a partner. Listen to the tape again, if necessary. (Note: The adjectives on the left may describe more than one memory.)

WHICH MEMORY IS	
Scary?	
Dramatic?	
Funny?	
Sad?	
Happy?	

Threads

I write because I'm filled with all the words I never spoke as a child.

Michael Nava, author

LEARNING STRATEGY

Center Your Learning: When you work in small groups, choose a specific task so you can focus more clearly.

D. DISCUSS

Answer the following questions about the photos and descriptions in groups of three. Student One asks the question, Student Two answers, and Student Three writes the answer. Change roles after each question.

Then report your answers to the class. Make sure your group has an answer for each of the following questions:

1. Which memory is about the **first time** a person did something?
2. In your opinion, which memory caused a **personal change?**
3. Which photo shows a memory from someone's childhood?
4. Which memory is about a surprise?
5. Which memory is very unusual?
6. Which memory is one that many people might have?

LEARNING STRATEGY

Forming Concepts: Seeing a picture in your mind of something you want to talk or write about will give you more ideas.

Interview

Visualize (close your eyes and see a picture in your mind of) some of your memories. Make the memories as detailed as possible. Think about them for a few minutes.

Now, work with a partner. Ask your partner about some of his or her unforgettable memories. Start with the following questions, and then add some of your own:

1. What is your funniest memory?
2. Can you remember something very scary that happened to you?
3. When were you sad? Why?
4. What special memory do you have from your childhood?

Quickwrite

Write about one of the memories you described to your partner in **Interview**. Write for ten minutes without stopping. Do not worry about grammar or spelling; just get your ideas on paper.

PART II

Language Expansion

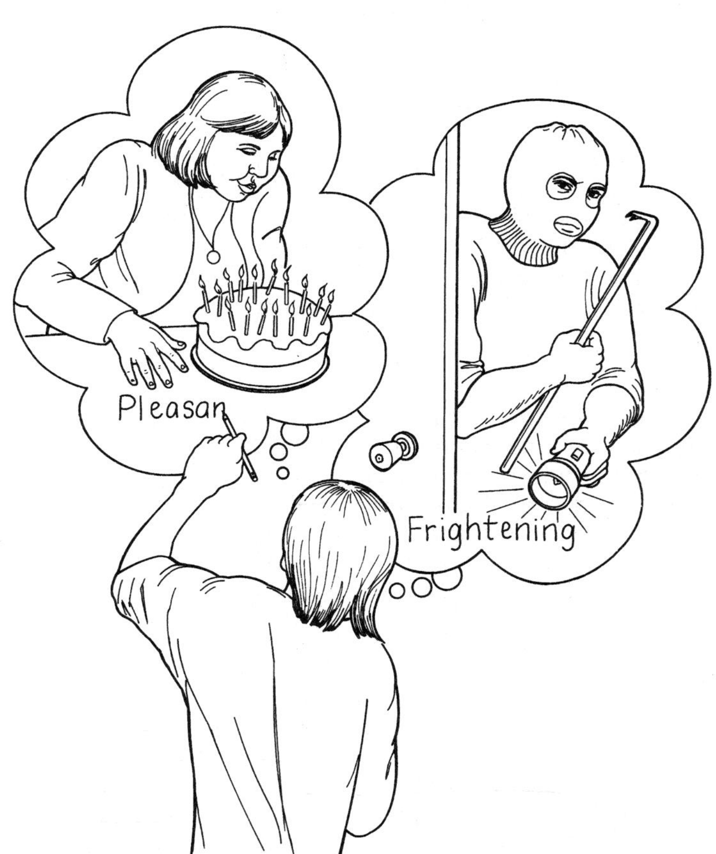

Threads

Memorial Day: American holiday devoted to honoring the memory of America's war dead.

LEARNING STRATEGY

Understanding and Using Emotions: When you become aware of other people's thoughts and feelings, you learn new things and get to know your classmates.

A. WORD LIST

Following are some words and expressions you can use to talk about memories. How many do you already know? In small groups, share the meanings you know. Give examples of words whenever you can. Talk about the difference between *frightening* and *frightened, embarrassing* and *embarrassed,* and *scary* and *scared*. Note that the words are organized into three columns. Can you guess why?

SUPER WORD LIST: MEMORIES

incident	frightening, frightened	to remember
event	memorable	to recall
the past	dramatic	to remind someone (of something)
journal (entry)	embarrassing, embarrassed	
detail	unforgettable	
	scary, scared	
	pleasant	

B. DETAILS

When you write about past events, it is important to include lots of specific details so the reader can understand exactly what happened and appreciate why it is so memorable for you. Look at the two paragraphs below. Read them and answer the questions.

Threads

A memory is what is left when something happens and does not completely unhappen.

Edward de Bono, British author

PARAGRAPH A

I'll never forget the first time I visited the countryside outside of Santa Fe, New Mexico with my family—it was just as beautiful as everyone said it would be. The area looks dry, but it rains every afternoon in the summer. We took many walks and saw a lot of interesting plants and rock formations. It's at a very high elevation and the air is nice. It's no wonder that so many famous artists settled there to work.

PARAGRAPH B

I'll never forget the first time I went to the countryside outside of Santa Fe, New Mexico with my family—it was just as beautiful as everyone said it would be. My mother and I took long walks. We noticed that even though it has a desert climate, it rains every afternoon in the summer. This makes the air clean and clear, and it brings out various shades of greenish-grey in the plants and trees. The vegetation contrasts with the reddish-brown of the rocks and hillsides it grows on. Due to the clean air, and perhaps the elevation, there's also a special kind of light that makes things shimmer—it's almost as though everything has a silver outline. It's no wonder that so many famous artists settled there to work—there's nothing like the magical light of northern New Mexico.

1. Which paragraph do you like the best? Why?
2. Which paragraph has more specific details?
3. Reread Paragraph B and *underline* as many specific details as you can. When you are finished compare notes with your neighbor. Did you find the same details?

4. Choose four details that you underlined in Paragraph B. Write the questions that they answer.

Detail: (The rain) brings out the various shades of greenish-gray in the plants and trees.	**Questions**: What do the plants and and trees look like?
Details:	**Questions**:
a. ______________________	______________________
b. ______________________	______________________
c. ______________________	______________________
d. ______________________	______________________

LEARNING STRATEGY

Forming Concepts: Study other people's writing to get ideas and improve your writing.

Read, Discuss, and Write About a Memory

A. READ ABOUT IT

Remember the refrigerator memory from Part I? Here is the rest of the story, "Trapped Under a Refrigerator." A student from Spain, studying English in the United States, wrote it for a class assignment. It was a childhood memory that made him laugh whenever he thought about it.

LEARNING STRATEGY

Forming Concepts: To make a reading passage easier to understand, think ahead and predict what comes next.

- Before you read, predict what you think will happen and why this event is so memorable for the writer.
- As you read, look for specific details and notice how the writer has used dialogue to make the incident come alive.

TRAPPED UNDER A REFRIGERATOR

by Antonio Farré

When I was a boy, I used to play with my brother in the kitchen of my house. We would climb on the refrigerator and jump off. We thought it was great fun. It made us feel big and brave.

2 One time I was up on the refrigerator and I jumped. When I landed on the floor, the refrigerator fell on top of me. I couldn't move. I was caught. My brother was frightened. He tried to lift the refrigerator, but he couldn't. He began to cry loudly, and when my mother heard him, she ran into the kitchen. When she saw that the refrigerator was on the floor and I was under it, she thought that I was dead and she began to scream and shout. Then my father came into the kitchen and said,

3 "What happened?"

4 My mother cried, "Look!", and pointed to the refrigerator.

5 And my father said, "I only see the refrigerator!"

6 My mother said, "Yes, but your son is **under** the refrigerator!"

7 I finally escaped with the help of everyone in my family. I didn't break any bones. I was only frightened. To punish me, my mother didn't let me have any ice cream that day. I still remember that incident because it was so frightening then, but it is so funny now.

B. WHAT DO YOU REMEMBER?

In small groups, answer these questions about "Trapped Under a Refrigerator."

1. Why do you think the writer chose this incident to write about?
2. What details do you remember?
   a. Approximately how old was the writer when this happened?
   b. Who was he with?
   c. Where did it happen?
   d. What happened?
3. The dialogue helps you understand how the people in the story were feeling. Reread the dialogue and complete the following sentences by underling **all** the appropriate adjectives.
   a. The brother was unconcerned frightened scared
   b. The mother felt worried frightened helpless happy
   c. The father was confused angry sad
4. Can you think of an incident in your past that was frightening at the time, but seems funny now?

C. WRITING CONVENTIONS: DESCRIBING A MEMORY

Answer these questions about the writing conventions in "Trapped Under a Refrigerator."

1. Does the title make you want to read the piece? Is it an interesting title?
2. What verb tense does the writer use?
3. Who tells the story?
4. How do you know who is talking in Paragraph 2?
5. These are the main ideas from Antonio's story. Put them in the correct order by numbering them from 1 to 3.

_______ What happened one time they played the game

_______ The results of the incident, and his feeling then and now

_______ A game the writer often played with his brother

6. How many of the following questions does the writer answer?
   a. When did the event happen?
   b. Where did it happen?
   c. Who was there?
   d. What happened?
   e. What did people say?
   f. How did people feel?

SUMMARY

- When you write about past events, an interesting title will invite the reader to continue with enthusiasm and curiosity.
- Since the events occurred in the past, the verbs are usually all in the simple past tense [*play→played*] or the past habitual tense [*play→used to play*].
- When writers describe a memory from their past, they use first person throughout. ["When **I** landed on the floor, the refrigerator fell on top of me. **I** couldn't move. **I** was caught."]
- When you write about past events, it is a good idea to include dialogue, that is, people's conversations. This helps the reader understand the characters better. It also makes your writing more dramatic. When you want to include conversation in your writing, remember to enclose anything someone says directly in quotation marks ("...") and when the speaker changes, move to the next line.
- To develop details in a description of a past event, ask and answer "Wh-questions": who, what, where, when, why, and how.

Threads

A good storyteller is a person who has a good memory and hopes other people haven't.

Irwin S. Cobb, American writer

PRACTICE WRITING

Use your ideas from your **Quickwrite** in Part I to write a new paragraph on one of your memories. Make sure you

- think of an interesting title
- pay attention to verb tense
- include some dialogue
- answer the wh-questions

PART III

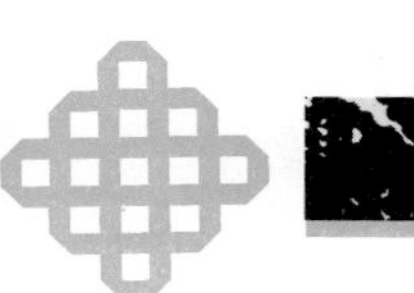

Gather Information and Write About a Memory

A. ORGANIZE AND DEVELOP YOUR IDEAS

Mindmapping is a useful way to record and organize ideas. A mindmap is a "picture" of ideas. There are many kinds of mindmaps. You can use a mindmap to help understand the ideas in something you have read or when you are preparing to write.

You use a **cluster** when you mindmap; a cluster is a group of idea categories. You can use it to help you remember different events from your past.

1. Here is an example of a cluster Antonio Farré started with before he wrote "Trapped Under a Refrigerator."

Unforgettable Events From My Past:

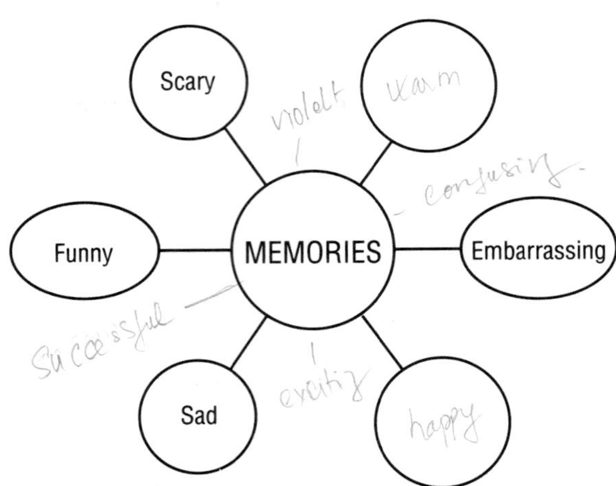

Can you think of other categories? Write them in the empty circles.

2. Now, take a look at Antonio's next step.

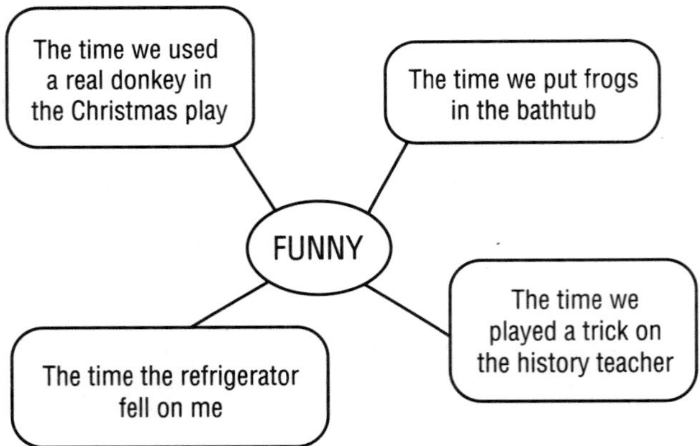

As you can see, he took one of the categories and gave examples for it. (You can do this for any category.)

LEARNING STRATEGY

Managing Your Learning: Organizing before you write makes the writing task easier and helps you generate ideas.

Now make your own cluster of unforgettable events. Start with "Memories", as Antonio did in Example 1. Then, take each of your categories and give at least three examples, as Antonio did in Example 2.

B. SHARE YOUR IDEAS

Work in small groups. Use the cluster you just made. Choose one of your memorable events and tell it to your group members. If you have a photo of the event, bring it. As you listen to each other's stories, ask wh-questions (who, what, when, where, why, how) to help each other think of descriptive details to make your stories more interesting.

C. PREPARE

Write a dialogue to go with your memorable event. Refer to the rules for writing dialogue in Part II on page 9. When you finish, exchange dialogues with a partner. Read and make suggestions. Rewrite any parts you feel you can improve.

D. WRITE!

Now you're ready to write.

1. Write about an unforgettable event in your life. Include descriptive details and dialogue.

After completing assignment 1, try the following for further practice:

2. Write about the quote at the beginning of the chapter. Explain what it means to you.

Unless we remember, we cannot understand.
—Edward M. Forster

Assess

A. REFLECT

On the Reflections of My Writing chart (See Appendix A), fill in the boxes for Chapter 1: Memories.

B. EXCHANGE

Exchange your paper with a classmate and answer these questions.

1. Are there any questions about the memory that your partner forgot to answer? (For example, who, what, when, where, how).
2. Find the dialogue. Is it clear? Do you know who is talking? Does it make the story interesting?

C. REWRITE

Rewrite your paper, or just the parts that your partner or teacher found to be incomplete or unclear. As you write, consider the answers to the questions in Exercise B, or any other recommendations your partner had.

D. LOOK AHEAD

Now, write **one thing** you would like to improve in the next writing assignment.

LEARNING STRATEGY

Managing Your Learning: Keep track of what you have learned and what you still want to work on, so you can become an independent learner.

I'm going to work on. . .

____

____

____

____

____

2

CHAPTER

A Person You Admire

You must look into people, as well as at them.
—Lord Chesterfield,
eighteenth century English statesman and writer

We sometimes see ourselves best by looking at others. People we respect and admire reflect the values we hold. In this chapter you will think and write about people you have known that you consider special.

PART I

Get Started

A. TAKE A LOOK

The following photos show people who have been important in the lives of six others. These photos emphasize special qualities each of these people have. Look at the pictures and think of at least one adjective to describe each person in the photos. Write your adjective or adjectives on the lines above the pictures.

a. ____________________

b. ____________________

c. ____________________

d. ____________________

e. ____________________

f. ____________________

B. LISTEN AND MATCH

Listen to the following descriptions of people. Work with a partner and match each description to the corresponding picture. Write the number of the description next to the photo.

C. BRAINSTORM

Make a list of at least five people you admire. These people can be friends or family members. They can be people you see frequently or people you haven't seen or talked to for a long time. Two of the people on your list can be famous people you have never met. Keep this list handy; you'll use it several times as you work through this chapter.

1. ______________________________
2. ______________________________
3. ______________________________
4. ______________________________
5. ______________________________

LEARNING STRATEGY

Forming Concepts: When you quickly write down what comes to mind, you're brainstorming, which helps you generate ideas and increase fluency.

Interview

Visualize your favorite person. Remember as many details about him or her as you can. Think about this person for a few minutes.

Work with a partner. Have your partner choose one of the people on the list from **Get Started.** Exercise C. Encourage your partner to say as much as possible about his or her special person. Start with the following questions, and then add some of your own:

1. How do you know this person?
2. What does this person look like?
3. What unique habits or behavior does this person have?
4. What do you admire about this person?
5. Why did you choose this person to talk about?

Quickwrite

Write about a person you admire. It can be about someone you know now or someone from your past. Write for ten minutes without stopping. Do not worry about grammar or spelling; just get your ideas on paper.

PART II

Language Expansion

A. WORD LIST

Following are some words and expressions you can use to describe people you admire. How many do you already know? In small groups, share the meanings you know.

Divide the remaining words among your group members and take turns teaching the new words to the group after looking them up in the dictionary.

Threads

Rick Hansen wheeled his wheelchair over 24,901 miles around the world in 1985.

SUPER WORD LIST 2: SPECIAL PEOPLE

relative	to care about
characteristic	to admire
personal quality	to respect
	to look up to

LEARNING STRATEGY

Remembering New Material: When you look for relationships between words and ideas, you remember more effectively.

B. DESCRIPTIVE ADJECTIVES

It is a good idea to review adjectives that describe people when writing about people you admire. You can divide these words into two groups, adjectives that describe physical characteristics (what people look like), and adjectives that describe personality (how people act around others). Read these adjectives with your group members:

Threads

A hero is no braver than an ordinary man, but he is brave five minutes longer.

Ralph Waldo Emerson, American essayist

SUPER WORD LIST 2A: A PERSON YOU ADMIRE

PHYSICAL CHARACTERISTICS

tall	short	stocky	strong	thin
heavy	skinny	fat	muscular	petite
attractive	good-looking	plain		

PERSONALITY CHARACTERISTICS

friendly	shy	open	reserved	happy
quiet	cheerful	warm		

1. Arrange the preceding adjectives in two different ways. First, put all the words that "go together" in a group. For example, *friendly* and *cheerful* have related meanings, so they go in the same group. Then, put the words in pairs of opposites. How many opposite pairs can you find? Feel free to add as many words as you can.

	RELATED	OPPOSITES
Examples:	friendly, cheerful	shy/open

2. Look at the following "mug shots" (photos the police use to find criminals). When the police are looking for criminals, they need exact descriptions of physical characteristics. Write physical descriptions for the police to help them find these criminals.

LEARNING STRATEGY

Remembering New Material: When you try to use words you've just learned in sentences, it helps you remember their meanings.

3. Choose a person from your list in **Get Started,** Exercise C. Describe his or her physical appearance and personality.

C. VISUAL DETAILS

When you think about a special person, what is it you "see"? Take a moment and imagine this person . . .

When you write about someone, you can show what he or she is like by describing characteristic actions or behaviors. You can begin by describing physical and personality characteristics (things *anyone* could see if they met this person), but your writing will be more interesting if you can add a description of what *you* see when you think of this person. The following poem describes what is special to the poet about her mother, and this is not what everyone might notice.

Mother's Hands, Mother's Eyes

And when you ask what I remember about her,
Don't ask about the cut of her clothes
Or the kind of work she did,
How she wore her hair
Or if she loved her husband.
Ask instead how her hands looked,
fingers long in the pale winter light,
nails lacquered red and gleaming,
tapping against the oilcloth
the morning after the Christmas dance.
Ask if the stories she told were true.
And, ask if her eyes, when she looked at me,
Ten years old in my pajamas,
Ask me if my mother's eyes were green and kind.

Marty Williams

1. In this poem, the poet describes her mother by telling the reader what to ask about her. What do you know about the poet's mother?
2. Now practice writing about things only *you* see when you think of a special person. Choose a person from your list in **Get Started**, Exercise C. Write about the characteristics that you notice. Make a list of these characteristics. Share this with the class.
3. Choose one of the special people from your list in **Get Started**, Exercise C. Write a poem like "Mother's Hands, Mother's Eyes." Tell the reader what questions to ask about your special person. Think of questions that tell the reader what you remember about your special person.

LEARNING STRATEGY

Overcoming Limitations: Trying a new form of writing helps you become a more fluent writer.

Read, Discuss, and Describe a Person You Admire

A. READ ABOUT IT

As adults, we often look back to our past and remember people who helped us or changed us or taught us something important. The following passage is by Robert Drechsler, a middle school teacher from San Francisco, who has written about his high school baseball coach.

Before you read, answer these questions:

1. What is a *coach*?
2. Who are the people we remember from our youth? Why do we remember them? Because they are kind? Mean? Frightening? Important?

3. Predict why you think Coach Keating was an important influence in the writer's life.

As you read, look for what the writer remembers about his coach. Try to identify how the writer helps you, the reader, "get to know" Coach Keating.

COACH KEATING: A MEMOIR

by Robert Drechsler

baseball fever: *public excitement about national and local baseball teams*
undefeated: *never lost a game*
arch-rival: *competitor*
swept up: *very excited*

1 It's October, and everyone has *baseball fever*. Our two local professional teams are in the World Series. Everyone is talking about baseball. Even our school's team, the Ben Franklin Wildcats, have just won their first game in two years, with a score of 13-5. My son's team is *undefeated* and has just beaten its *arch-rival* in a close and exciting contest. I'm feeling *swept up* by everything happening at once.

eternity/linked: *a very long time/connected*
pattern: *model*

2 But whenever I think of baseball, I must go back in time to think about my first baseball coach, Jim Keating. He was the coach for an *eternity* at my high school. His name was *linked* with winning and honor for as long as I can remember. He is the person upon whom I *pattern* my life as a coach.

Threads

China's Fu Mingxia won the Women's Platform Diving World Championship in 1991 when she was 12 years old.

3 I remember the first time I met Coach Keating. We were at a summer sports camp that I attended after the eighth grade. He was a medium-built man with *sandy brown* hair and large, bony fingers—fingers that had probably seen too many *foul tips* bounce off them. I especially remember the bushy hair on his *knuckles*. He usually wore plain *khaki* pants and a *checkered* shirt. All in all, he was not a very *flashy* guy.

light brown

balls that are hit high, difficult to catch, and out of bounds/joints in fingers/ green-brown/pattern of squares/noticeable

4 At the sports camp, we played baseball, ran miles, shot basketballs, and had a good time. There were two good athletes there, myself and a kid named "Dirty" Al Gallagher, who later played baseball for the San Francisco Giants. One time we had to run an obstacle course in the gym. We had to run over equipment, under horizontal bars, through tires, and around partitions. I remember doing the course once in about 42 seconds. Dirty Al did it in 41.5 seconds. Coach Keating asked if anyone would like to try it again. I said, "yes." I ran around the course as fast as I could, and was doing well until I came to the parallel rails—here I had to balance myself for about twenty feet as I walked across two parallel bars high off the ground. I immediately fell off and had to start again. I had lost time, but when I finished, Coach looked at his watch, looked again, and announced: "Forty-one point five seconds." I shared the prize of a candy bar, even though I was sure my time was slower. I'll never forget that because it showed me what Coach Keating stood for: a man who rewarded effort, a man who had time for all kids, and a man who wanted kids to succeed.

5 When I got to know him better and was on his team year after year in high school, I learned that he was always ready to help the kids, as a coach, a mentor, or a father figure. He was fair. If you *screwed up*, you'd get a good *tongue-lashing*, but he'd never *humiliate* you. He proved that hard work and *perseverance* would *pay off*. He often had the baseball team out on the practice field, *sloshing* around in the rain, doing a long workout. Things like rain never bothered Coach Keating. He believed you should "work hard—it'll pay off." It usually did, even if you didn't win a championship. But you learned the value of hard work.

made a mistake

disciplinary lecture/make you look foolish/patience/ result in success/walking around in water

6 Coach Keating went on to fight many battles in his life. He won one championship after another at our high school. But the last battle he lost. I read in a recent alumni newsletter that Coach Keating died after a long struggle with cancer. When I saw that, a little bit of my youth seemed to slip away. I *reflected* a bit and thought to myself, "Here's a man I am proud to have known, a man who inspired me to be the best athlete I could be, a man that has shown what a coach could do with a team, a man that I would never be embarrassed to say I truly loved."

thought

B. WHAT DO YOU REMEMBER?

Answer these questions about the reading. Work in small groups.

1. What did Coach Keating look like when the writer first met him?
2. The writer tells us that Coach Keating's appearance was not so memorable. What was memorable about Coach Keating?
3. What details do you remember about the reading?
   a. During which season does the writer always remember his sports coach?
   b. How old was the writer when he met his coach?
   c. Which sports did Coach Keating train students for?
   d. Who was "Dirty" Al Gallagher?
   e. What happened when the writer and Dirty Al were running an obstacle course?
   f. What did Coach Keating teach the writer?

LEARNING STRATEGY

Remembering New Material: A quick review increases your understanding and helps you remember what you have learned.

C. WRITING CONVENTIONS: DESCRIBING PEOPLE

Answer these questions about the writing conventions in "Coach Keating: A Memoir."

1. What is the first paragraph about? What tense does the writer use in this paragraph?
2. What tense does the writer use in Paragraphs 2 to 6?
3. What main quality does the writer emphasize about Coach Keating?
4. What is the purpose of Paragraph 4?
5. What is the purpose of the last paragraph?

Threads

On August 6, 1926, Gertrude Ederle was the first woman to swim across the English Channel.

SUMMARY

- The writer describes some activities and his emotions during the current baseball season in the present (and present perfect tense) to get you, the reader, involved in the subject. You can begin to write about the past by writing about the present.
- The rest of the essay is in the past tense, because the writer is describing past events and a person who is no longer alive.
- What Drechsler remembers most about Coach Keating is that he showed kids that if they worked hard, they would succeed. When you write about a special person, think of one quality to emphasize and illustrate.
- The writer uses an anecdote (brief story) in Paragraph 4 to illustrate the coach's ability to inspire and teach young people. Use an anecdote to emphasize important qualities in a person you admire.
- In the last paragraph, the writer expresses his feelings about Coach Keating. It reminds the reader of how special his coach was and it concludes the piece on a personal and poignant note.

PRACTICE WRITING

Use your ideas from your **Quickwrite** in Part I to write a new paragraph about a person you admire. As you write,

- pay attention to verb tense
- use descriptive language
- include an anecdote to illustrate one of the person's special qualities

Gather Information and Describe a Person You Admire

A. ORGANIZE AND DEVELOP YOUR IDEAS

In the last chapter you learned how to make a **mindmap** with your ideas before writing. A mindmap helps you record and organize your ideas. In this chapter, you are going to practice another way of generating ideas and organizing them. This method is similar to making an **outline**. We will call it a **vertical mindmap**.

In a vertical mindmap, you make notes on all the categories of ideas you want to write about. For example, when you write about someone you admire you want to include:

- how you know this person
- what the person is like
- what you do (or did) together
- why you admire this person (or why you chose to write about him or her)

List these categories on the left side of a piece of paper; use the space on the right side for taking notes and jotting down additional details before writing your first draft.

A vertical mindmap helps you divide ideas into paragraphs from the beginning of the writing process. You can add or omit categories depending on what you want to write. Remember that you can do a vertical mindmap for any writing topic, not just on someone you admire.

Here is the left side of a vertical mindmap for "Coach Keating".

• a snappy introduction that relates to the way we spent time together	*October, baseball is everywhere, World Series. I remember Coach Keating.*
• how we know each other	Summer sport camp.
• description: what I notice(d) about this person	Size, hair, hands, clothes. Coach style, interaction with kids.
• something we did together	I obstacle course.
• why I admire this person	proud, love, learned hard work

Work with a partner. Go back to the essay on Coach Keating on page 20. Find the information for each paragraph that goes with the categories on the left. Jot them down in note form on the lines to the right of the vertical mindmap.

B. SHARE YOUR IDEAS

Do a vertical mindmap for the topic you wrote about in Chapter 1. (See Chapter 1, page 10.) Complete both left and right sides of the cluster. Show your mindmap to a partner. Discuss your mindmaps and make recommendations for improvement.

C. PLAN

Practice doing a vertical mindmap for two people you admire. You can use the Coach Keating categories as they are, or you can change them. Show them to a partner. Did you use the same categories, or different ones? Discuss and make recommendations for improvement.

D. WRITE!

Now you are ready to write. As you write, keep in mind the goal(s) you set in Chapter 1.

1. Write about a person you admire. It should be someone you know or knew well and can describe in detail. Here are some specific suggestions:

- Someone who taught you an important lesson
- A childhood playmate
- A grandparent or aunt or uncle who paid particular attention to you
- A friend or classmate who showed you something new
- Someone who could do something you could not do
- A parent who helped you do something for the first time
- Someone who is particularly generous, successful, kind, funny, etc.

You can refer to photographs, letters, or objects to stimulate memories and specific details about this person. Plan your writing by doing a vertical mindmap.

After completing assignment 1, try the following for further practice:

2. Write about the quote at the beginning of the chapter. Explain what it means to you.

You must look into people, as well as at them.
—Lord Chesterfield

Assess

A. REFLECT

On the Reflections on my Writing chart (see Appendix A), fill in the boxes for Chapter 2: A Person You Admire.

B. EXCHANGE

Exchange your paper with a classmate and answer these questions.

1. Are there any questions about the special person your partner forgot to answer?
2. Find the description of physical characteristics. Is it clear? Can you really see what this person looks like?
3. Does the writer give you a good idea of what he or she sees in this person that is special?
4. Can you think of an incident that shows what the special person is like?

C. REWRITE

Rewrite your paper, or just the parts that your partner or teacher found to be incomplete or unclear. As you write, consider the answers to the questions in Exercise B, or any other recommendations your partner had. Also, check to see that you have improved the area(s) you wanted to work on at the end of Chapter 1 (See Chapter 1, page 12).

D. LOOK AHEAD

Now, write **one thing** you would like to improve in the next writing assignment.

I'm going to work on. . .

____

____

____

____

____

Threads

Nobel Peace Prize Winners: Mother Teresa of Calcutta, India in 1979; Lech Walesa of Poland in 1983; the Dalai Lama of Tibet in 1989.

3

CHAPTER

Names

The beginning of wisdom is to call things by their right name.
—Chinese proverb

Our names "define" us. They identify us, our family, and our culture. We "become" our names. They begin to reflect who we are. In this chapter you will learn about other people's names and have an opportunity to write about your own.

PART I

Get Started

A. LISTEN AND WRITE

Listen to some people talk about their names. Take notes as you listen. Listen a second time and write the speaker's names on the following lines. Do not worry about correct spelling. (Also, some of these people have a formal name and a nickname; write both, if possible.)

Speaker 1. ______________________________

Speaker 2. ______________________________

Speaker 3. ______________________________

Speaker 4. ______________________________

Speaker 5. ______________________________

B. LOOK AND MATCH

Match the following drawings to the name descriptions you just have just heard. Use your notes to help you do this. Work alone, and then share your answers with a partner when you have finished.

C. REMEMBER

With a partner, answer these questions about the people and their names. There may be more than one answer to some of the questions.

1. Which people have nicknames? How did they get them? 3, 4, 5
2. Which speakers are named after family members? Do they like their names? 2, 4
3. Who was named for his father's hopes? 1
4. What is unusual about one person's name? Who has something unusual about his or her name? 4, 2.
5. Which person changed his or her name recently? Why? 5

Interview

Think about your name. What do you see or feel when you think about your name? Think about it for a few minutes.

be haite

LEARNING STRATEGY

Understanding and Using Your Emotions: When you discuss your feelings with a classmate, you build friendship and understanding.

Now, work with a partner. Ask your partner about his or her name. Start with the following questions, and then add some of your own.

1. What is your name? What does it mean?
2. Where did your name come from?
3. Who named you?
4. How do you feel about your name? If you could change your name, what would your new name be?

Quickwrite

Write about how you got your name or nickname. Or, if you could change your name, write about what your new name would be. Write for ten minutes without stopping. Do not worry about grammar or spelling; just get your ideas on paper.

PART II

Threads

Florida gets its name from Spanish, meaning "feast of flowers."

Language Expansion

A. WORD LIST

Following are some words and expressions you can use to talk about names. How many do you already know? In small groups, share the meanings you know.

Look up the new words and use them in sentences.

SUPER WORD LIST 3: NAMES

custom	traditional	honor (verb and noun)	to be named for
tradition	common		to be named after
namesake	unusual		to be named by

B. PASSIVE VOICE

When you write about names, you will probably want to refer to your birth and how you got your name.

Look at these two sentences.

She **was born** in the year of the horse.
She **was named** for her grandmother.

These expressions, *was born* and *was named,* require putting the verb in the **passive** rather than the usual **active** voice.

The passive voice indicates that the subject is the **receiver,** not the **doer**, of the action. Verbs in the passive voice follow the subject and are made up of a form of *to be* and the past participle. Here is the formula:

SUBJECT + *TO BE* + PAST PARTICIPLE

1. Practice using the passive voice by answering these questions.

- Where were you born?
- What was happening in the world when you were born?
- Were you named for a special person?

2. There are three prepositions you can use after **to be named:** *for, by,* and *after*. They may have different meanings. Draw lines to match each phrase in the list on the left with its correct meaning on the right.

I was named *for* my aunt.	My aunt gave me my name.
I was named *by* my aunt.	I have my aunt's name.
I was named *after* my aunt.	I have my aunt's name.

Which two expressions have the same meaning?

Read, Discuss, and Write About a Name

A. READ ABOUT IT

The following reading is a work of fiction by Sandra Cisneros, an American writer who grew up in the Spanish-speaking section of Chicago. Cisneros has written many short stories about people from her childhood neighborhood. Cisneros' writing is simple and direct. She sometimes writes the way people think or speak to themselves—that is, her sentences are not always complete. Cisneros has written "My Name" to describe the feelings of a young girl named Esperanza, and you will notice that the writing "sounds" as if a young girl is talking.

LEARNING STRATEGY

Forming Concepts: Being a "cultural ambassador" develops international understanding.

- Before you read, answer these questions:
  1. What are some common Spanish names for girls? If you need help, think of famous women from Spanish-speaking countries, or characters from movies, novels, and songs. In addition, if there are

any Spanish-speaking students in the class, they can help answer this question.

2. Why do some people dislike their names? Think of as many reasons as you can, and then share your ideas with the class.

- As you read, look for images (word pictures) that the writer uses to describe her feelings about her name.

MY NAME

by Sandra Cisneros

1 In English my name means "hope". In Spanish it means too many letters. It means sadness, it means waiting. It is like the number nine. A *muddy* color. It is the Mexican records my father plays on Sunday mornings when he is shaving, songs like *sobbing*.

when dirt mixes with water it becomes this color/crying intensely

2 It was my great-grandmother's name and now it is mine. She was a horse woman too, born like me in the Chinese year of the horse—which is supposed to be bad luck if you're born female—but I think this is a Chinese lie because the Chinese, like the Mexicans, don't like their women strong.

3 My great-grandmother. I would've liked to have known her, a wild horse of a woman, so wild she wouldn't marry. Until my great-grandfather threw a *sack* over her head and carried her off. Just like that, as if she were a fancy *chandelier*. That's the way he did it.

bag

fancy hanging light that hangs from the ceiling and often has many small light bulbs

4 And the story goes she never forgave him. She looked out the window her whole life, the way so many women sit their sadness on an elbow. I wonder if she made the best with what she got or was she sorry because she couldn't be all the things she wanted to be. Esperanza. I have inherited her name, but I don't want to inherit her place by the window.

5 At school they say my name funny as if the *syllables* were made out of tin and hurt the roof of your mouth. But in Spanish my name is made out of a softer something, like silver, not quite as thick as sister's name—Magdalena—which is uglier than mine. Magdalena who at least can come home and become Nenny. But I am always Esperanza.

word or part of word containing a vowel sound or a consonant that acts as a vowel

6 I would like to *baptize* myself under a new name, a name more like the real me, the one nobody sees. Esperanza as Lisandra or Maritza or Zeze the X. Yes. Something like Zeze the X will do.

a religious ceremony in which a child becomes a member of a religion and is given a name

B. WHAT DO YOU REMEMBER?

In small groups, answer these questions about "My Name."

1. Who is Esperanza named after?

LEARNING STRATEGY

Remembering New Material: Finding and reviewing key words helps you remember important ideas.

2. Use these "key words" to remember and retell three facts about the great-grandmother's life.

   a. horse **b.** sack **c.** window

3. Why was the great-grandmother "wild?"
4. Think of one word to describe the great-grandmother's life.

LEARNING STRATEGY

Remembering New Material: Briefly state what you have learned in order to clarify your understanding and remember the material.

5. Esperanza compares the English and Spanish versions of her name. Use the chart below to recall the author's explanation of the meaning and pronunciation of her name in the two languages.

ESPERANZA	English	Spanish
Meaning	______	______
	______	______
Pronunciation	______	______
	______	______

6. Does Esperanza like her name? Why or why not?
7. By reading "My Name," you begin to know Esperanza. Circle four adjectives from the list below that describe her.

independent	lazy	bilingual	passive
indifferent	honest	curious	

8. Esperanza has mixed feelings about her name. That is, there are things she likes and dislikes about it. List what she likes and dislikes in the chart below.

HOW ESPERANZA FEELS ABOUT HER NAME	
What she likes	What she dislikes
______	______
______	______
______	______

9. What is the new name Esperanza would like to have? Why do you think she would like this name? What does "baptize" mean?
10. How does Esperanza describe the Chinese and Mexican attitude towards women? What is your opinion of her description?
11. How many "word pictures" or images could you find? Make a list with the class.

C. WRITING CONVENTIONS: WRITING ABOUT A NAME

Threads

There are almost 3,000 Wongs in the San Francisco telephone book.

Answer these questions about the writing conventions in "My Name."

1. What is the *literal* meaning of Esperanza? (That is, what is the English translation of the word?) What is another meaning the name has for the young girl? (What are her *associations* with the name?)
2. Complete the following sentences:
   a. Esperanza was named for ______________________.
   b. Esperanza was named by ______________________.
3. In which paragraphs does the writer refer to how she feels about the name Esperanza (either directly or indirectly)?
4. Cisneros develops paragraphs around answers to the following questions:
   a. How is your name pronounced?
   b. Who were you named for?
   c. What would your new name be?
   d. What does your name mean?
   e. What was your namesake like?

Put these questions in the order Sandra Cisneros answers them in "My Name."

LEARNING STRATEGY

Forming Concepts: Analyzing the order of points you have learned helps you verify relationships between ideas.

SUMMARY

- When you write about names, you can include the literal meaning as well as associations the name has.
- It is not necessary to include everything you know about your name. Pick the details that will make your writing powerful. Try to develop one main idea about your name.
- Be sure to support your opinion with lots of reasons.
- When writing about your name, organize your ideas in paragraphs that explain the *meaning* of the name, its *origin, feelings* associated with the name, and possible *new names*. You can order your paragraphs in the same way Cisneros did or in a different way.

PRACTICE WRITING

Use your ideas from your **Quickwrite** in Part I to write a new paragraph on how you got your name or nickname. Make sure you include the literal meaning of your name (if you know it); and develop one main idea about your name.

PART III

Gather Information and Write About a Name

LEARNING STRATEGY

Personalizing: Applying your new knowledge to personal situations and settings reinforces what you have learned in class.

A. RESEARCH

Collect information about your name. You may want to interview some relatives about how you got your name. You may also want to learn more about the person you were named after. Consider answering these questions too.

1. Is your name often mispronounced? How do you feel when people mispronounce your name? What does it sound like when people mispronounce it?
2. Were you named after someone? Do you admire the person you were named after? Would you like to live like this person?
3. What is a new name you would like to have that captures your personality and goals?

Threads

The full name of Los Angeles is "El Pueblo de Nuestra Señora la Reina de los Angeles de Porciuncula."

B. ORGANIZE AND DEVELOP YOUR IDEAS

Now organize the information you have collected. Make an outline of the main ideas you want to develop about your name. The boxes in the chart on page 36 indicate paragraphs. Write the main idea of each paragraph at the top of the box and fill in each box with explanation and details.

meaning of name.
literal meaning: (hope)
associations (muddy color)

Meaning of name
TRANG - Solemn, elegant (Trang nhã) DAI: (Đài các) Aristocratic or Noble TRANG-DAI: - place on high tower.

Who was I named by who?
- My parents

…er name

…me sake.
…nunciation
…n feeling's
…n experiences)
…nge to another
…ne? Why?
…n
…ning/association
…ck name -

Name Sake.
- general use for woman. -

C. WRITE!

Now you're ready to write about names. As you write, keep in mind the goals you set in Chapters 1 and 2.

1. Write about your name. Include one or more of the topics about names you have seen in this chapter:

- its origin
- feelings associated with the name
- how people pronounce the name

2. Write about a nickname. Choose your own or another person's nickname. Answer the same questions you would answer if you were writing about someone's formal name.

After completing assignment 1 or 2 or both, try the following for further practice:

3. Write about the quote at the beginning of the chapter. Explain what it means to you.

   The beginning of wisdom is to call things by their right name.
   —Chinese proverb

4. Combine ideas from a previous chapter with ideas from this chapter. For example, write about the name of someone you admire (Chapter 2).

Threads

Bob Dylan, a famous rock musician, changed his name from Robert Zimmerman.

Assess

A. REFLECT

On the Reflections on my Writing chart (See Appendix A), fill in the boxes for Chapter 3: Names.

B. EXCHANGE

Exchange your paper with a classmate and answer these questions.

1. How many paragraphs are there? What is the main idea of each paragraph?
2. If the writer talks about the meaning of a name, does he or she discuss the associations the name has?
3. Are the opinions in the paper supported with lots of reasons?

C. REWRITE

Rewrite your paper, or just the parts that your partner or teacher found to be incomplete or unclear. As you write, consider the answers to the questions in Exercise B, or any other recommendations your partner had. Also, check to see that you have improved the area(s) you wanted to work on at the end of Chapter 2 (see Chapter 2, page 25).

D. LOOK AHEAD

Now, write **one thing** you would like to improve in the next writing assignment:

I'm going to work on. . .

____

____

____

____

____

Learning Styles

I hear and I forget, I see and I remember,
I do and I understand.

—Chinese proverb

There are many ways to look at learning. How we learn best might depend on our personalities, what we learned as children in school, or how we've copied our parents. Knowing how we learn can make us better learners—and make learning easier and more fun. In this chapter, you will look at several different learning styles and write about the kind of learning that works best for you.

PART I

Get Started

A. TAKE A LOOK

The following photos show people learning the word *stretch* in three different ways. Look at the pictures and describe the differences with your classmates.

1.

2.

3.

If you didn't know the meaning of the word *stretch* and you wanted to learn it, which of the situations above would make you the **most comfortable** and help you learn the word? Share your answer and the reasons for your answer with a classmate.

LEARNING STRATEGY

Understanding and Using Emotions: Be aware of any tension as you do various language exercises, and try to relax your muscles.

B. GUESS AND DO

What kind of learner do you think you are? Look again at the pictures on page 40. First, make a guess. Write "s" if you think situation 1 works best for you, "h" for situation 2, and "d" for situation 3. Write your guess here: ______. (You will learn what "s", "h", and "d" mean in a few minutes.)

Now take the following survey to see if your guess is right. Read these sentences. Then respond by checking the appropriate line to indicate what is always, sometimes, or never true for you.

WHAT'S YOUR LEARNING STYLE?	ALWAYS TRUE (3)	SOMETIMES TRUE (1)	NEVER TRUE (0)
1. I like to talk alot when I'm learning something.	______	______	______
2. I remember names, song lyrics, and new words easily.	______	______	______
3. I can follow oral directions easily.	______	______	______
4. I'm always moving: nodding, tapping, shaking, wiggling.	______	______	______
5. When I talk, my hands are as important as my voice!	______	______	______
6. I have a habit of touching things I walk past.	______	______	______
7. I'm good at noticing visual details; I like to play "Find the Hidden Picture" games.	______	______	______
8. I like to see what it is I'm going to learn.	______	______	______
9. I hate reading books that have no pictures.	______	______	______

In order to find out which kind of learner you are, put an "h" beside sentences 1, 2, and 3. They indicate a learner who learns best by **hearing** what he or she will learn (auditory). Put an "d" beside Sentences 4, 5, and 6. They indicate a learner who learns best by **doing** what he or she will learn (kinesthetic). Finally, put a "s" beside sentences 7, 8, and 9. They indicate a learner who learns best by **seeing** what he or she will learn (visual). Add points for each of the different learning styles. (An 'always true' answer is worth 3 points, 'sometimes true' is 1 point and 'never true' is 0.) The learning style with the most points is probably your learning style preference. If none of the learning styles got high scores, then perhaps you favor a combination of learning styles. Were you surprised? Share your results with your classmates.

Threads

The first thing education teaches you to do is walk alone.

Alfred Aloysius Horn

Interview

Ask a classmate these questions about learning. Then add some additional questions of your own.

1. Do you enjoy learning?
2. What kinds of things do you learn fast or easily?
3. What kinds of things do you do to learn better?
4. Which learning styles listed above are new to you?
5. Which kind of learning works best for you?

Quickwrite

Think about a time when your learning was really successful. What were you studying? Where were you? Who were you with? What did the teacher do? What activities were included? Write about this time and provide as many details as you can. Write for ten minutes without stopping. Do not worry about grammar and spelling; just get your ideas on paper.

PART II

Language Expansion

A. WORD LIST

Following are some words and expressions you can use to talk about learning styles. How many do you know? In small groups, share the meanings you know.

Try to identify **roots** (or stems) for the words with an(*). Identifying the root may help you discover the word's meaning.

SUPER WORD LIST 4: LEARNING STYLES

mode	auditory*	kinesthetic*	visual*	competitive*
strategies	cooperative*	memorize*	analytic*	relational*
task				

B. STEMS AND AFFIXES

One way to increase your vocabulary is to learn the parts of words.

Prefixes come at the beginning of words and **suffixes** come at the end. They attach to **stems,** the basic part of the word. Study some common word parts with a partner, and then practice using them in words and sentences.

PREFIXES	Meaning	STEMS	Meaning	SUFFIXES	Meaning
in-	not	auto	self	-able	capable of
re-	again	bio	life	-er	one who
inter-	between	dict	say	-ly	in this way
multi-	many	geo	earth	-ful	full of
un-	not	logy	study	-ous	full of
mis-	wrong	meter	measure	-tion	condition

Read, Discuss, and Write About Your Learning Style

Threads

There were over 40 million students in public schools in the U.S. in 1989-90.

U.S. Department of Education

A. READ ABOUT IT

Read the following selection on learning styles from a textbook that two language teachers wrote. Because they wrote it for education students, you may find that the passage includes more difficult words and is more formal than the reading selections in previous chapters.

LEARNING STRATEGY

Personalizing: As the writers have done here, keep your audience's personal needs and interests in mind when you write.

- Before you read, answer these questions: What are the five senses? Is there a relationship between your senses and learning? What could it be?
- As you read, try to find examples of general statements and specific details. This is going to be a difficult reading. Before you begin, close your eyes and think of one of your favorite places or people. Think about your breathing, too.

LEARNING STYLES

by Rebecca L. Oxford
and Robin C. Scarcella

methods
measurement in any one direction
having to do with bodily senses/desire or liking
concerning the body/having to do with noticing and understanding

1 Language learning styles are the *general approaches* students use to learn a new language. These are the same styles they use in learning many other subjects and solving various problems. There are four *dimensions* of language learning styles. We will only discuss one dimension here: *sensory* preferences. Students' *preferences* for a particular sensory approach accounts for very significant differences between language learners. Sensory preferences refer to the *physical* and *perceptual* learning channels with which the student is the most comfortable. There are three major sensory preferences and these are visual, auditory, and hands-on (movement and touch).

things that cause a reaction
support

2 Visual students need to see what is asked of them. They like to read, look at pictures, and they are good at noticing visual details. They can also be distracted by *visual stimuli:* a new sign, a bird outside the window, or a person walking past the classroom. For them, lectures, conversation, and oral directions without any visual *backup* can be confusing or difficult to understand.

verbal and/or nonverbal communication

3 Auditory students, on the other hand, are comfortable without visual input and therefore enjoy lectures, conversations, and oral directions. They are excited by classroom *interactions* in role-plays and similar activities. They learn best by talking. They remember names, song lyrics, and language patterns easily. They are usually excellent readers and good singers. They sometimes, however, have difficulty with written work.

can be felt, touched, or held

4 Hands-on students like lots of movement and enjoy working with *tangible* objects, building projects, and learning with flashcards. They have difficulty sitting at a desk for long periods of time. They prefer to have frequent breaks and move around the room. They learn best through their muscles and are often tapping or drumming when still. Hands-on learners touch objects they walk past and use lots of facial expressions and gestures when they talk.

showed in a concrete way
not considered important

5 How do sensory preferences relate to cultural learning styles? A recent study *demonstrated* that ESL students vary significantly in their sensory preferences. Students from Asian cultures, for instance, are often highly visual, with Koreans being the most visual. Other studies have found that Hispanics are frequently auditory, and Japanese are very nonauditory. ESL students from a variety of cultures are hands-on learners, perhaps more than we would at first imagine. This is probably because kinesthetic learning is encouraged in these cultures. In America, where hands-on learning has been largely *devalued,* teachers are beginning to see the benefits of making learning more "active".

B. WHAT DO YOU REMEMBER?

In small groups, answer these questions about the reading selection.

1. Are sensory preferences the only way we look at learning styles? NO
2. Refer to the last sentence in the first paragraph. Rewrite it using your words. (What do sensory preferences mean to you?)
3. What is one thing visual students do well?
4. In what activity would an auditory student succeed?
5. How can a hands-on student learn best?
6. Now give examples of one exercise or activity with which a visual, auditory, and hands-on learner could have trouble.
7. Think of your classmates. Can you identify a visual, auditory, and hands-on learner in your current class?
8. What has a recent study found about Korean, Hispanic, and Japanese students?
9. How are some American teachers changing?
10. Use the information from the reading selection to help your teacher plan a class by including activities for all three kinds of learners: visual, auditory, and hands-on. Would the following activities help a hands-on, auditory, or visual learner? Complete the following chart by putting a check (✓) in the appropriate column.

LEARNING STRATEGY

Forming Concepts: Using charts or checklists helps you understand better.

ACTIVITY	HANDS-ON	AUDITORY	VISUAL
1. Display vocabulary words on flashcards			✓
2. Perform a puppet show	✓		
3. Trace letters in the air to learn correct spelling			✓
4. Memorize a poem		✓	
5. Use pictures to introduce vocabulary			✓
6. Write directions for every task			✓
7. "Act out" actions to learn verbs	✓		
8. Use different colors to indicate nouns, verbs, adjectives			✓

C. WRITING CONVENTIONS: WRITING ABOUT LEARNING STYLES

Answer these questions about the writing conventions in "Learning Styles."

1. Look at the first paragraph of "Learning Styles." This paragraph defines learning styles and sensory preferences. Which of these is most general? Which is most specific?
2. Look at the first sentences in paragraphs 2, 3, and 4. Are these sentences **more** or **less** general than the sentences that come after?

LEARNING STRATEGY

Managing Your Learning: Having an expectation of what you will hear or read can make you a more active and independent learner.

3. Look at the last paragraph. Did you expect to read about cultural learning styles or was this introduced in the first paragraph?
4. When the writers give specific examples of what visual, auditory, and kinesthetic learners do **well,** do they also give examples of what each kind of learner **does not** do well? Make a list to help you answer the question.

	HANDS-ON	AUDITORY	VISUAL
Do Well	________	________	________
	________	________	________
	________	________	________
Don't Do Well	________	________	________
	________	________	________
	________	________	________

SUMMARY

- This selection is more formal and academic than the pieces we have read in previous chapters. It is organized according to a pattern that you will find in college textbooks and essay writing courses. The introductory paragraph is arranged from general to specific. That is, the authors define the most general topic, language learning strategies, and then explain the less general topic, sensory preferences. The final sentence in this paragraph is the main idea of the selection. This sentence is called the **thesis statement**.

LEARNING STRATEGY

Forming Concepts: To understand how to communicate appropriately, observe differences between formal and informal language and communication patterns.

- In paragraphs 2, 3, and 4, the body paragraphs, the first sentence is the most general sentence. This is called the topic sentence. Note that specific examples explaining the topic sentence make up the rest of the paragraph.
- The final paragraph, or the conclusion, takes the topic, sensory preferences, and applies it to something new. Since the writers knew that readers would be interested in cultural learning styles, they added this to keep the readers' interest. In your conclusion, you can apply your topic to something new too.
- When you write about learning styles, give lots of specific examples. Examples will make your writing interesting and convincing.

PRACTICE WRITING

Use your ideas from your **Quickwrite** in Part I to write a body paragraph on one of your learning experiences. Make sure you have a topic sentence and some specific examples.

PART III

Gather Information and Write About Your Learning Style

A. RESEARCH

Keep track of your learning for a day. Take notes on the learning activities you do. Indicate whether the activities are for visual, auditory, or hands-on learners. Record your feelings and rate of success as you do the activities. Make a chart like the one below. This will help you collect more information about your learning style.

ACTIVITY	HANDS-ON	AUDITORY	VISUAL	FEELINGS	DID YOU LEARN?
Drew pictures of new vocabulary	✓			Confident	Yes

B. PLAN AND ORGANIZE

Now organize your information by taking notes in the chart. Follow the model of "Learning Styles" by Scarcella and Oxford. Put your most general information in the introduction and make sure your main idea is the last sentence of the first paragraph. Plan your writing by answering the questions:

Introduction	Most general idea: What are different learning styles?	__________
Thesis Statement	Main Idea: What kind of learner are you?	__________
Paragraph 1 Topic Sentence	What's one reason you know you're an X learner?	__________
Paragraph 2 Topic Sentence	What's a second reason you know you're an X learner?	__________
Paragraph 3 Topic Sentence	What's a third reason you know you're an X learner?	__________
Conclusion	How does your learning style relate to other activities?	__________

Threads

For 1990-91, the average cost for tuition at a private, 4-year college in the U.S. was $9,391.00.

U.S. Department of Education

C. PREPARE

Write an introductory paragraph that would explain differences in learning styles in your own words. End this paragraph with a statement about your learning style.

D. WRITE!

Now you are ready to write. Choose one of the following topics. As you write, keep in mind the goals you set in previous chapters.

1. Write about your learning style preference.
2. If you can make a general statement, write about a group's learning style. This could be a culture, a specific age group, a family, etc.
3. Explain the quote at the beginning of this chapter.

I hear and I forget, I see and I remember, I do and I understand.
—Chinese proverb

LEARNING STRATEGY

Managing Your Learning: Choosing your own topic helps you take charge of your learning.

4. Do research on any aspect of learning that interests you and write about your findings. For example, you might be interested in other learning theories, or in the people who discovered and wrote about these learning theories.
5. Combine ideas from a previous chapter with ideas from this chapter. For example, write about the learning style of someone you admire (see Chapter 2).

Assess

A. REFLECT

On the Reflections on My Writing chart (see Appendix A), fill in the boxes for Chapter 4: Learning Styles.

Threads

On average, United States libraries loan 3,360,827 books every day.

Digest of Educational Statistics (1990)

B. EXCHANGE

Exchange your paper with a partner and answer these questions:

1. Has the writer begun with a general introduction and ended the first paragraph with a statement of the main idea?
2. Are there general sentences followed by examples for each of the body paragraphs?
3. Are there enough examples? Indicate where an example either is not clear or is missing.

4. Has the writer concluded the writing with an idea that makes the topic interesting and relevant to the reader?
5. Are there any comments or recommendations you can make that might improve this paper?

C. REWRITE

Rewrite your paper or just the parts that your partner or teacher found to be incomplete or unclear. As you write, consider the answers to the questions in Exercise 6, or any other recommendations your partner had. Also, check to see that you have improved the area(s) you wanted to work on at the end of Chapter 3 (see Chapter 3, page 38).

D. LOOK AHEAD

Now, write **one thing** you would like to improve in the next writing assignment.

LEARNING STRATEGY

Managing Your Learning: Keeping a language learning diary helps you keep track of your successes and makes you a more independent learner.

I'm going to work on. . .

____

____

____

____

____

CHAPTER 5

Places

There's no place like home.
—Dorothy, *The Wizard of Oz*

When you write about a place you know well, you may discover new things about yourself. In fact, many famous writers have described places where they have lived or visited. These places have inspired them to express important feelings. In this chapter, you are going to describe a special place and explain how it makes you feel.

PART I

Get Started

LEARNING STRATEGY

Understanding and Using Emotions: You can take intelligent risks like guessing without feeling worried or anxious.

A. TAKE A LOOK

The following photos show a variety of places. Look at the pictures and try to guess what each place is. Then think of two or three words that describe each place.

______________ **b.** ______________ **c.** ______________

______________ **e.** ______________ **f.** ______________

B. LISTEN AND MATCH

Listen to the following descriptions of places. In small groups, match each with the picture it goes with. Write the number of the description next to the photo.

C. REMEMBER

In your groups, answer these questions about the place descriptions you have just heard.

1. What does Francisca do in her kitchen?
2. How does the library make Tomo feel?
3. What did Stephane do in New Mexico last summer?
4. What does Brigitta probably do at the beach near her home?
5. Why does Mary like to do homework at the cafe?
6. How does Oscar describe the Museum of Modern Art?

Interview

Visualize your favorite place. That is, form a picture of it in your mind. Make your picture as detailed as possible. Think about your favorite place for a few minutes.

Now, work with a partner. Ask your partner about a place he or she particularly likes. Start with the following questions, and then add some of your own:

1. Do you have a favorite place?
2. What does it look like?
3. What do you usually do in this place?
4. How does this place make you feel?

Threads

The temple of Horyu-ji in Naro, Japan, is the world's oldest wooden structure, built in 670 A.D.

Quickwrite

Write about your favorite place. It can be indoors or outdoors—a place where you work, play, study, or do nothing. Describe it. Write for ten minutes without stopping. Do not worry about grammar or spelling; just get your ideas on paper.

PART II

Language Expansion

A. WORD LIST

Following are some words and expressions people use to describe places. How many do you already know? In small groups, share the definitions you know.

Give examples of each starred (*) word.

SUPER WORD LIST 5: PLACES

quiet*
noisy*
modern*
old-fashioned*
crowded*
cluttered*
dark*
clean*
light*
peace,* peaceful
comfortable*
airy*
spacious
to spend time
to get peace and quiet

B. SO + ADJECTIVES

You can describe a place by using *so* and an adjective, and a result clause. You use this construction for emphasis. It gives the reader a clear picture of the *value* (or degree) of the adjective you have chosen. For example:

The beach is *so cold*, you can't go swimming.
(How cold is it? It's too cold for swimming.)

It's *so quiet* on the third floor *that* I can hear myself think!
(How quiet is it? It's quiet enough to hear something you can't normally hear!)

so + adjective, (*that*) + result clause

The word *that* at the beginning of the result clause is optional. (You do not *have* to use it.)

Threads

"U" in the Caroline Islands has one of the shortest names of any town or city in the world.

Here are some more examples:

- The cafe is so noisy, it helps me concentrate on my school work.
- I'm up so high, I have a view of the whole city.
- My apartment is so crowded, I can't get any peace and quiet!

1. Match the following *so* phrases on the left with the result clauses on the right. (There may be more than one result clause for each *so* phrase.)

The beach is so windy	(that) I can't get any work done.
The library is so quiet	(that) you can easily get lost.
My dorm room is so noisy	(that) you can hear a pin drop.
The city is so big	(that) you can't have a conversation.
The woods near my home are so peaceful	(that) you can hear yourself think.

2. Make up *so . . . (that)* sentences about the following places:

- my parents' house
- the cafe in my neighborhood
- the park
- the school cafeteria
- the school library

3. Make up five *so . . . that* sentences about your favorite place. You can write sentences about the place you described in Part I, **Quickwrite**.

Threads

Angel Falls in Venezuela is the highest waterfall in the world with a total drop of 3,212 ft. (979 m).

Read, Discuss, and Describe a Place

A. READ ABOUT IT

Many famous writers have written about places that are special to them. One of these writers, Annie Dillard, an America born in 1945, describes a favorite place near her Connecticut home in her book *A Pilgrim at Tinker Creek.* Read the following excerpt, a description of Tinker Creek. (A creek is a small stream.) Do not worry if you do not understand all of the words; just try to guess their meanings. We have given explanations of some of the most difficult ones in the margin.

- Before you read, imagine that you are walking alongside a creek. What kinds of plants do you see? What kinds of animals do you see? What else do you see? How do you feel? Share your ideas with the class.

LEARNING STRATEGY

Managing Your Learning: When you have something to focus on as you read, you improve your understanding of the reading selection.

- As you read, try to answer this question: How does the description of Tinker Creek make you *feel*? What words or expressions give you this feeling?)

A PILGRIM AT TINKER CREEK

By Annie Dillard

When I slide under the barbed wire fence, cross a field, and climb over a sycamore trunk *felled* across the water, I'm on a little island shaped like a tear in the middle of Tinker Creek. On one side of the creek is a steep forested bank; the water is swift and deep on that side of the island. On the other side is the level field I walked through next to the *steers'* pasture; the water between the field and island is shallow and *sluggish*. In summer's low water, *flags* and *bulrushes* grow along a series of shallow pools cooled by the lazy current. Water *striders* move across the surface film, *crayfish* walk slowly along the slit bottom eating filth, frogs croak and stare, and shiners and small *bream* hide among roots from the green *heron's* eye. I come to this island every month of the year. I walk around it, stopping and staring, or I straddle the sycamore log to read. Today I sit on dry grass at the end of the island by the slower side of the creek. I'm drawn to this spot.

that has fallen

cows

slow

(both) kinds of plants

an insect/an animal that lives i
fresh water; it looks like a lobste

kinds of fish/a bird

From *Pilgrim at Tinker's Creek,* Annie Dillard. Harper's Magazine Press, New York 1974, pp. 4–50.

B. WHAT DO YOU REMEMBER?

In small groups, answer these questions about Dillard's description:

LEARNING STRATEGY

Forming Concepts: When you draw a picture of something, it can help you understand it better.

1. Draw a picture of the island in the middle of Tinker Creek.
2. What is the water like on one side of the island? What is it like on the other side?
3. Describe in your own words what the insects, fish, and animals at Tinker Creek are doing.
4. What does Dillard do at Tinker Creek?

5. How do you think the writer feels when she's at Tinker Creek? Calm? Nervous? Tired? Energetic? Find an adjective that describes her feeling, then list the words and expressions from the excerpt that support your opinion.

   Adjective: ____________________

   Examples: ____________________

   ____

   ____

   ____

6. What does the last sentence mean? What does *to be drawn* to a place mean?

Threads

Hudson Bay in northern Canada has a shoreline of 7,623 miles (12,295 km).

C. PRACTICE: WRITING ABOUT FEELINGS

Places often make you feel a certain way. When you describe a place, you can state directly how it makes you feel. ("The library is so quiet, it makes me feel calm.") You can also state feelings indirectly: you can describe things associated with the place that suggest feelings. This is what Dillard does.

For example: ". . .the water . . . is *sluggish*." ". . .the *lazy* current . . ." "Sluggish" and "lazy" suggest slow movement and calm. In this exercise, think of places that make you feel a certain way. List as many places as you can for each of the feeling:

LEARNING STRATEGY

Understanding and Using Emotions: Organizing your ideas in a chart or a list helps you to see the relationship between feelings and places.

NERVOUS	HAPPY	CALM	CREATIVE	ENERGETIC	UNCOMFORTABLE
	My bedroom		*the library*	*the beach*	

In small groups, talk about why these places create these feelings for you. Think about how the people and things you find at these places make you feel the way you do.

D. WRITING CONVENTIONS: PLACE DESCRIPTIONS

Answer these questions about the writing conventions in the excerpt from *A Pilgrim at Tinker Creek.*

1. Find the sentence that compares the island to a *tear*. What word or expression does Dillard use to make the comparison?
2. Dillard uses a lot of adjectives in her description. List them, and say what they describe.

ADJECTIVE	THING IT DESCRIBES
forested	bank
steep, lazy	bank, current
swift, small	current, bream
deep, low	water/creek, water.
shallow, dry	water, grass
sluggish, level	current, field.
little, green,	island, heron.

3. How many animals does Dillard talk about in her description? List them. How many plants does Dillard talk about? List them.

ANIMALS	PLANTS	WHAT THEY LOOK LIKE/ WHAT THEY ARE DOING

After you list them, write what they are doing or what they look like in the third column.

4. What tense does Dillard use in her description of Tinker Creek? Give three examples.

SUMMARY

- Comparing a thing to something else can give the reader a clear picture in a place description. You can use Noun X *is like* Noun Y to make a comparison.
- You can also give your reader a clear picture of a place by using descriptive adjectives.
- Another way to describe a place is to talk about things, animals, or people you find at the place. You can describe them with adjectives and/or you can say what they are doing.

Threads

Mobile, Alabama, averages 64.64 inches of rain a year, the highest in the U.S.

Statistical Abstract of the U.S.

- Use the *present tense* in a description. It helps readers feel *closer* to the place you are describing, as though they are in that place with you.

LEARNING STRATEGY

Managing Your Learning: When you work with others to solve a problem, you can learn from them.

PRACTICE WRITING

Work in small groups. Listen to the following recordings. You will hear three recordings of sounds, only. They are sounds you hear in particular places. You will not hear people talking.

The first time you listen, try to decide where the place is. Then listen two or three more times. As you listen, take notes on what you hear. When you finish, discuss the recordings with the group. Do you agree or disagree on what you heard?

Then work alone and write short descriptions (one paragraph) of each place the sounds are coming from. As you write, make sure your descriptions include the following:

- a comparison
- some adjectives
- some people, things, or animals you might find in the place
- the present tense

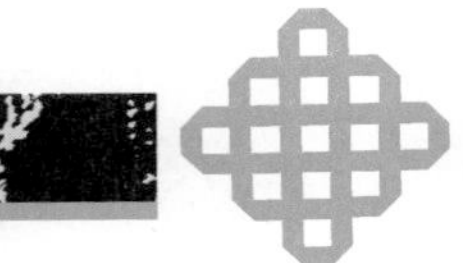

PART III

Gather Information and Describe a Place

A. RESEARCH

Choose a place to write about. Go to this place at least one more time and really *look* at it, even if it is a place you spend a lot of time in everyday.

Take notes on this place:

- What does it look like?
  —take a picture of it
  —sketch it
  —draw a map of it

- What things, animals, or people do you find there?
- What are they doing?
- What do you do in this place?
- What or who does this place make you think of?
- How does the place make you feel?

B. SHARE YOUR IDEAS

Bring your notes to class. In small groups, take turns describing out loud the place you have chosen to write about. Bring a picture, if you can. Ask and answer questions; make sure you describe your place clearly, including what you do and how you feel there.

Threads

Moscow has the most public transportation passengers of any city in the world, 2.426 trillion per year.

International Union of Public Transport, Brussels

C. FREE-WRITE

Write a short description of the place. Just describe how it looks. Do not worry about what you do there or how you feel yet. Use the notes you took in Exercise A. When you finish, exchange your paper with a classmate. Read and make suggestions. Then, rewrite any parts you feel you can improve.

D. WRITE!

Now you are ready to write. Choose one of the following topics. As you write, keep in mind the goals you set in previous chapters.

1. Write a description of a place that creates one of the following feelings:

- nervous
- happy
- calm
- creative
- energetic
- uncomfortable

Include how the place looks, important things, animals, or people you find there, what you do there, and how the place makes you feel. You can state feelings directly, or indirectly.

2. Write a description of the place in this painting by Edward Hopper. Include:

- what the place looks like to you
- the people or things in the picture and what they are doing
- the general feeling the picture gives you

Edward Hopper, American, 1882-1967, Nighthawks, oil on canvas, 1942, 76.2 x 144 cm, Friends of American Art Collection, 1942.51.

After completing assignments 1 and 2, try the following for further practice:

3. Explain the quotation at the beginning of the chapter:

There's no place like home.
—Dorothy, *The Wizard of Oz*

Dorothy is the girl from the American story (and film), *The Wizard of Oz,* who wants to run away from home. After a series of adventures far from her home, she realizes that all she wants to do is go back home again. Do you agree or disagree with Dorothy? What is your home like? How does it make you feel?

LEARNING STRATEGY

Managing Your Learning: When you connect new material with material you already know, you take control of the learning process.

4. Combine ideas from a previous chapter with ideas from this chapter. For example, write about an unforgettable event that happened in a special place (Chapter 1), write about how a place got its name (Chapter 3), or describe how a special place makes learning easier (Chapter 4).

Assess

A. REFLECT

On the Reflections on My Writing chart (see Appendix A), fill in the boxes for Chapter 5: Places.

B. EXCHANGE

Exchange your paper with a classmate and answer these questions:

1. Are there any comparisons in your partner's description? If not, would a comparison help?
2. List some of the adjectives your partner uses. Do they give you a clear idea of the place? Of the people, animals, or things in the place?
3. How does your partner describe the feelings associated with the place? Directly? Indirectly? Does your partner clearly explain these feelings?
4. What verb tense does your partner use?

C. REWRITE

Rewrite your paper, or just the parts that your partner or teacher found to be incomplete or unclear. As you write, consider the answers to the questions in Exercise B, or any other recommendations your partner had. Also, check to see that you have improved the area(s) you wanted to work on at the end of Chapter 4 (see Chapter 4, page 50).

D. LOOK AHEAD

Now, write **one thing** you would like to improve in the next writing assignment:

I'm going to work on. . .

____

____

____

____

____

Threads

Three of the world's most densely populated cities are in China—Shenyang, Tianjin, and Chengdu.

U.S. Bureau of the Census

CHAPTER 6

Music As Personal History

Music is the universal language of mankind.
—Henry Wadsworth Longfellow,
19th century American poet

Songs often reflect popular culture. They also tell us something about ourselves—they help us remember friends, places, adventures, and struggles we may have had. In fact, the memories a favorite old song recalls can be so clear that hearing it is almost like watching a movie of your life and times. In this chapter, you will explore music and its associations for you.

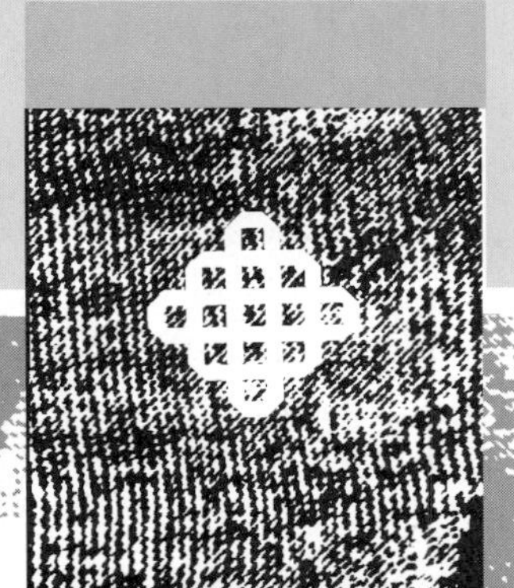

PART I

Get Started

A. TAKE A LOOK

The following photos are of some popular international and American musicians from the last 30 years. Their faces and their music are well-known in most parts of the world. How many of these musicians can you identify?

LEARNING STRATEGY

Personalizing: If you have a favorite story, some objects or photographs that relate to what you are studying, share them with classmates to increase everyone's understanding of the topic.

B. MATCH

Now look at the following list of song titles. In small groups, complete the following activity by matching the song with the musician. Do you have any of these recordings? If so, bring them to class and play them for your classmates.

SONG		MUSICIAN	
Beat It!	Material Girl	The Beatles	Elvis Presley
Like a Rolling Stone	Yesterday	Bob Dylan	Bob Marley
You Gotta Pray	Hound Dog	Michael Jackson	Madonna
No Woman, No Cry	I Can't Get No Satisfaction	The Rolling Stones	Hammer

LEARNING STRATEGY

Managing Your Learning: Concentrating when you are communicating helps you learn faster.

C. LISTEN

Listen to the following lecture by Ellen White, an expert on popular music. She discusses the musicians you identified at the beginning of this chapter. After you listen, fill in the chart that follows.

In small groups, complete the following chart with the information you've listened to.

MUSICIAN	BECAME POPULAR	KIND OF MUSIC	FAMOUS FOR	NOTES
__________	__________	__________	__________	__________
__________	__________	__________	__________	__________
__________	__________	__________	__________	__________
__________	__________	__________	__________	__________
__________	__________	__________	__________	__________
__________	__________	__________	__________	__________
__________	__________	__________	__________	__________
__________	__________	__________	__________	__________

Interview

Ask your partner these questions and then add some questions of your own.

1. What kind of music do you like to listen to?
2. Name four of your favorite musicians, two from the past and two from the present.
3. Name four of your favorite songs, two from the past and two from the present.
4. Which of the musicians you've heard about in this chapter is the most interesting to you? Why?
5. Your own questions: ____________________

____

____

Quickwrite

LEARNING STRATEGY

Forming Concepts: To generate ideas before you write, take some time to "warm-up" your senses by listening, seeing, smelling, tasting, and feeling what the topic suggests to you.

Close your eyes. Let your favorite song play in your head. What do you feel? What do you remember? Who do you think of? What do you see in your mind when you hear this song? Now write about a song you like. If you can, include information about the musician, the lyrics, and what the song means to you. Write for ten minutes without stopping. Do not worry about grammar or spelling; just get your ideas on paper.

Language Expansion

A. WORD LIST

Following are some words and expressions people use to describe music and its associations. Get together with your classmates and share definitions you know.

LEARNING STRATEGY

Remembering New Material: Arrange words and ideas in categories of related meanings to help you learn and remember them.

Threads

Alan Freed, a disc jockey from Cleveland, Ohio, is generally credited with inventing the term "rock & roll."

Organize the words into semantic groups (words that are related).

SUPER WORD LIST 6: POPULAR MUSIC

rhythm	rock	reggae	beat	to popularize	romantic
instruments	tune	guitar	piano		classical
drum	flute	jazz	ballad		
lyrics	rock and roll	idol			
pop	rhythm and blues				
orchestra					

LEARNING STRATEGY

Remembering New Material: Learn by heart features of the language that do not follow rules.

B. SPELLING

By now you have probably noticed that English spelling is irregular and unpredictable. Some words in this chapter, like *rhythm, lyrics,* and *orchestra,* are particularly difficult to spell. It is a good idea to keep a special list of words that do not follow regular spelling rules or are a particular problem for you.

In the meantime, here are some spelling rules to review for words that **do** follow the rules:

Threads

Studies show that cows produce more milk when they hear jazz.

Lectionary of Music (1989).

Rule 1: When you cannot remember how to spell a word with *ie,* remember that *i* comes before *e* except when it's **after** *c.*
Rule 2: If you want to make a word that ends in *s, ss, zz, ch, x* or *sh* plural, add *es* and pronounce it as an extra syllable.
Rule 3: To make a word that ends in a consonant and *y* past tense, change the *y* to *i* and add *ed.*

Now practice applying these rules by correcting the misspelled words in these sentences.

1. Maria couldn't beleive that she received first prize for her piano solo.
2. Some churchs have large organs.
3. The hillbilly musician's shirt matchs his pants.
4. They hurryed so they wouldn't miss the rock concert.
5. They asked for classical music when they got marryd.

Read, Discuss, and Write About Your Associations With a Song

A. READ ABOUT IT

The selection you will read was written by T. C. Huo, an immigrant from Cambodia who is studying creative writing at an American university. He majored in English in college, and wrote this piece shortly after graduating.

- Before you read, share with your classmates what you know about political events in Laos, Thailand, and Cambodia since the 1970s. Refer to the map and locate Nongkhai and the Mekong River.

- As you read, pay attention to parts where the writer describes the song he is listening to and parts where he describes what it makes him think about.

THE SONG SENT ACROSS THE MEKONG

T. C. Huo

1 The male voice singing to his love on the other side of the water was familiar to many ears—including mine, when I was in the refugee camp. The radio played it. The *jukebox* played in it. In the camp as well as in downtown Nongkhai, customers of the coffee house fed coins to the jukebox to hear the singer sending his love across the Mekong to the woman he had left behind—a Vietnamese or a Lao farm woman in a straw hat and sarong, a brown-faced woman who stands in the mist by the river bank and looks through the mist across the Mekong to the border—to Nongkhai, Thailand. She doesn't know what has happened to her lover: whether he is safe, whether he has left the refugee camp and gone to a third country, America or Australia, or France, whether he has married. She can't hear his song.

jukebox: a machine found in public places that plays music when a coin is dropped in

2 Ten years later, in America, listening to the song on a tape, I see this man. The cassette is more than ten years old. Almost all the songs in it have begun to *blur:* voices thickened, dragged out, twisted. But as I hear this song, the male *vigor* in it is still as clear as ten years before when I first heard it in the camp. Hearing this voice, listening to the tune (that sad tune), a young man, whose brown face and thick, dark eyebrows reminded me of the inky brush of the iron-faced judge in the courtroom in the Chinese movies, springs from my head, flips a somersault, leaps onto the Mekong river bank, and is now standing *astride,* barefoot, by the water, his trousers (dark indigo, inky) rolled to his knees, his shirt sleeves (the same color as the trousers) rolled up to his elbows.

blur: become unclear
vigor: strength
astride: across

3 He calls her name. He doesn't know what has happened to her. That night he turned his back on her, walked out of the door. If the young man had made it across the border why couldn't he have brought her along? There were difficulties and impossibilities, *financial* and otherwise, that were stronger than his *vow* of love. Getting caught or gunned down by the Pathet Lao. Drowning. It seems right that the song omits why the young man would leave his woman behind. There were bachelors in the camp, many of them young men by themselves without family and without money. These men swam across the river, and if they had girlfriends, their girlfriends either

financial/vow: regarding money/promise

couldn't swim at all or couldn't swim the whole distance. So these men swam across the river to be bachelors.

4 Many women let their men go while they stayed and waited, either because they could not swim or even if they could, it was inconceivable that they be on their own in the refugee camp—how could they manage? Many women had to stay behind.

5 Not my mother. She didn't wait. To this day I still don't know what made her, or why she would, cross the river with my seven-year-old sister. They left my father without his knowledge. They left home for the *Land of Smiles.* What *puzzles* me is that she would take such a serious matter upon herself without consulting my father, the head of the household, and leave the country by herself keeping her thoughts from him. Had he known them, he would have seen to the matter, he would have pre-arranged a passage.

America/confuses

6 My friends and their families all crossed the border together and entered the refugee camp together. Other families, four or five members more than mine, big families, had reached Thailand safely. It does not make sense that it was hard for my family, a family of four members, not counting me, to *flee* the country together. It is hard for me to accept that.

escape from

7 My mother's body was never found. I see her flowing southbound, passing villages, passing under villagers' eyes, passing from one province to the next, kilometers and kilometers away from home. By the time my father and the rescue team arrived, a day or two later, they were too late: she had flowed into Cambodia.

8 My mother had even passed the singer by the bank at the Thai side of the river. As he was singing about how much he missed his loved one who remained in Laos, my mother was being turned and pushed by the current ten feet away from him. In the middle of the song, he saw a tree trunk—or a bundle of clothing—uncertain as to which way to drift.

9 My sister's body was found. The search for my mother: small-scaled. It was all my father could do. Having found my sister, he and a few of his friends kept on with the search. It couldn't go on too long if my mother would not surface. She was somewhere else. In the camp, I had thought that since she was not found, she must have been saved. She was somewhere along the river.

10 And I was in America, listening to the singer send his love across the water.

B. WHAT DO YOU REMEMBER?

In small groups, answer these questions about "The Song Sent Across the Mekong."

1. What kind of song is Huo talking about?
2. Was the singer famous in Huo's country? How do you know?
3. Where was Huo when he first heard the song?
4. Describe in your own words the subject of the song. What does Huo wonder about the young man in the song?
5. The song reminds Huo of an incident in his personal life. What was that incident?
6. How does Huo feel about the incident he remembers when he hears that song? What kind of memory does the song recall for him?

C. WRITING CONVENTIONS: A SONG AND ITS ASSOCIATIONS

Answer these questions about the writing conventions in "The Song Sent Across the Mekong."

1. In "The Song Sent Across the Mekong" the writer goes back and forth describing the music he hears and the memory or association he has with the music. Go through the selection again and put an "s" next to the sections that refer to the song, and put an "a" next to the sections that refer to the association or memory.
2. There are many different aspects of a song a writer can choose to describe. Put a circle around the things Mr. Huo describes in "The Song Sent Across the Mekong."

tune	the lyrics
instruments it features	rhythm
where he first heard it	who listens to it
why it is popular	feelings expressed in song

3. Go back to the selection and underline the verbs in the *past present* tense.
4. Make a list of the different **colors** the writer uses to describe his associations with "The Song Sent Across the Mekong."
5. Make a list of some of the feelings the writer has.

SUMMARY

- When writing about a song and its associations, you can organize your writing so that information about the song comes first and your associations with it come after, or you can do what Huo does and go back and forth between the song and his associations.
- You can choose to write about several aspects of a song. Choose the areas that you know about and the ones that interest you. Choose from these categories:

tune	the lyrics
instruments it features	rhythm
where you first heard it	who listens to it
why it is popular	feelings expressed in song

- Use the **past present** tense (*had* + past participle) to describe something that happened **before** a time in the past that is already established.

For example: Before I started playing the piano, I had studied the violin.

- Use sensory details to make your description of associations with a song more vivid. Write about what you see, hear, smell, or taste when you hear the song.

Threads

The world's largest rock concert was on July 21, 1990 by Pink Floyd on Potsdamer Platz in Berlin, Germany.

- Because of the emotional power of music, your associations probably include feelings. Describing your feelings makes your writing more personal.

PRACTICE WRITING

Use your ideas from your **Quickwrite** in Part I to write a new paragraph on a song you like. Include as many sensory details as you can and write about your feelings.

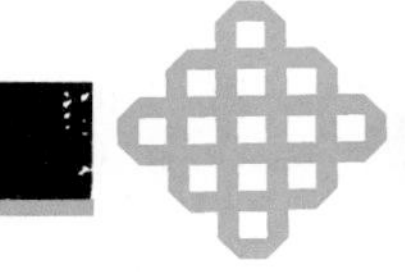

PART III

Gather Information and Write About Your Associations With a Song

A. RESEARCH

Collect information about one of your favorite songs. Listen carefully to the song. Write out and think about the lyrics. Then ask other people what they know about it. You may also want to read some cassette, CD or record covers, read a newspaper or magazine review, or interview a musician or someone who works at a music store.

LEARNING STRATEGY

Managing Your Learning: Consider alternative ways of communicating in speech and writing, so you can choose the best approach.

B. PLAN

Now organize your information arranging it in two different ways. In the first way, describe the song at the beginning, and then write about its associations for you. In the second way, go back and forth describing the song and its associations. Take notes in the chart below.

PLAN #1	PLAN #2
The Song	The Song
The Song	Its Associations
Its Associations	The Song
Its Associations	Its Associations

C. PREPARE

Choose the organizational pattern you prefer for writing about your associations with a song. Then write the one part that you already have a lot of notes or information for. When you finish, exchange your paper with a classmate. Read and make suggestions. Then, rewrite any sentences you need to make this part clearer.

Threads

Top songs:

1956 **"Hound Dog"** **Elvis Presley**
1962 **"The Twist"** **Chubby Checker**
1964 **"I Want to Hold Your Hand"** **The Beatles**
1968 **"Hey Jude"** **The Beatles**

D. WRITE!

Now you are ready to write. Choose one of the following topics. As you write, keep in mind the goals you set in previous chapters.

1. Write about a song and the associations it has for you.
2. Write about a musician and the associations she or he has for you.
3. Choose some lyrics from a favorite song, explain what they mean, and write about the associations they have for you.
4. Explain the meaning of the quote at the beginning of the chapter.

Music is the universal language of mankind.
—Henry Wadsworth Longfellow,
19th century American poet

After completing assignments 1-4, try the following for further practice:

5. Combine ideas from a previous chapter with ideas from this chapter. For example, write about a song that deals with memories (Chapter 1), a person's name (Chapter 3), or a special place (Chapter 5).

Assess

A. REFLECT

On the Reflections on My Writing chart (See Appendix A), fill in the boxes for Chapter 6: Music as Personal History.

B. EXCHANGE

Exchange your paper with a classmate and answer these questions:

1. Has the writer given you enough information about the song she or he has chosen to write about? Would you like to know anything else about it?
2. Does the writer have positive or negative associations with the song? Is it clear? Why?
3. Has the writer included enough sensory details?

2. Does the writer have positive or negative associations with the song? Is it clear? Why?
3. Has the writer included enough sensory details?
4. Has the writer described his or her feelings?

C. REWRITE

Rewrite your paper or just the parts that your partner or teacher found to be incomplete or unclear. As you write, consider the answers to the questions in Exercise B or any other recommendations your partner had. Also, check to see that you have improved the area(s) you wanted to work on at the end of Chapter 5 (see Chapter 5, page 63).

Threads

Madonna's full name is Madonna Louise Veronica Ciccone.

D. LOOK AHEAD

Now, write **one thing** you would like to improve in the next writing assignment.

I'm going to work on. . .

____

____

____

____

____

CHAPTER 7

Celebrations

We eat whenever life becomes dramatic: at weddings, birthdays, funerals, at parting and at welcoming home, or at any moment which a group decides is worthy of remark.

—Margaret Visser,
from *The Rituals of Dinner*

People everywhere celebrate the significant moments of their lives, such as birthdays, weddings, and holidays. These celebrations reflect the values and beliefs of our cultures. So studying important events and the ways in which people celebrate them helps us understand ourselves and others better. In this chapter, you are going to discuss and write about your favorite celebration, and explain the meaning or purpose of the celebration.

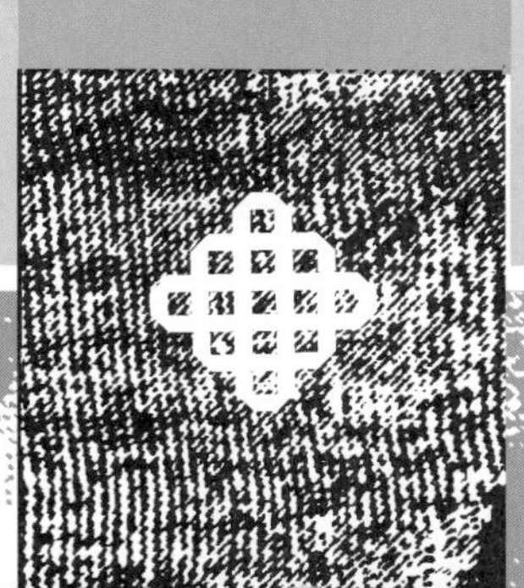

PART I

Get Started

A. TAKE A LOOK

Look at these photos. They show celebrations in different countries. Work with a partner. Try to guess what is happening, the country the celebration takes place in, and the name of the celebration.

a. ______________ b. ______________ c. ______________

d. ______________ e. ______________ f. ______________

B. LISTEN AND MATCH

Listen to the following descriptions of the celebrations in the photos. With your partner, match each description with the picture it goes with.

LEARNING STRATEGY

Forming Concepts: When you brainstorm, list ideas rapidly to improve your fluency and become a creative thinker.

C. REMEMBER

In the following chart, you will see the names of each of the celebrations pictured. Some of these celebrations take place in many parts of the world; we have given one location for each. With your partner, answer this question: Where else in the world do these celebrations take place?

Now, fill in the following chart on the celebrations you have just read about. Make a check in all the columns that describe the celebrations to the left.

Threads

"Ceremony is the smoke of friendship."

Chinese Proverb

Celebration	Special Clothing or Costumes	Special Meals or Foods	Presents	Entertain-ment or Dancing	Decorations
Halloween, United States					
Carnival, Venice					
Chinese New Year, San Francisco					
Wedding, Egypt					
Birthday, United States					
Quince Años, El Salvador					

Interview

Think about your favorite holiday in as much detail as possible. Then, work with a partner. Ask your partner about his or her favorite celebration. It can be a holiday, a birthday, a wedding, or other ceremony. Start with the following questions, and then add some of your own:

LEARNING STRATEGY

Understanding and Using Emotion: Sharing your feelings with someone else helps you discover what you really think and feel.

1. What is your favorite celebration? Why is it your favorite?
2. What is the purpose of this celebration?
3. What do you usually do for this celebration?
4. Can you visualize an event associated with this celebration? What sounds do you associate with the celebration? What smells do you associate with it?
5. Do you prepare any special foods for this celebration?
6. Your questions:

____

____

____

____

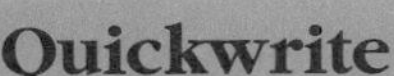

Quickwrite

Write about a holiday or a celebration. It can be an event you celebrate in your native country, or one from another country or culture. Write for ten minutes without stopping. Don't worry about grammar or spelling; just get your ideas on paper.

PART II

Language Expansion

A. WORD LIST

Following are some words and expressions people use to talk about holidays and celebrations. How many do you already know? In small groups, share the definitions you know.

Give examples of each starred (*) word.

SUPER WORD LIST 7: CELEBRATIONS

celebration	ball	to bring luck
symbol*	rite of passage	to insure
feast	period of,	to dress up
evil spirits	a time of (e.g. meditation)	to play tricks (on)*
costume*	traditional*	
mask	elaborate	
	traditionally	

B. EXPLAINING THE MEANING

When we talk about celebrations, we often explain the meaning of the celebration, or of the events and objects associated with it, such as food or costumes. Take a look at these examples from Exercise B, Part I:

- The dragon and fireworks scare away evil spirits and *ensure* a happy new year for all.
- In our culture, red *symbolizes* prosperity.
- To mark the new season, we clean our houses from top to bottom.

You can use these expressions to talk about the meaning or purpose of something:

X **is a symbol of** Y	explains what something means.
X **ensures** Y **To** + infinitive, **we** + sentence }	explain the purpose of something

Here are some more words and expressions for explaining the meaning and purpose of celebrations:

symbolizes	the celebration includes . . .
emphasizes	X is based on
invites	
means	
ensures	
celebrates	
marks	X is a time for/of + noun.
signifies	

LEARNING STRATEGY

Remembering New Material: Finding and circling new words in context helps you remember their meanings.

1. Reread the descriptions of celebrations in Exercise B, Part I. Find and circle all the expressions the speakers use that explain meaning and purpose.
2. Rewrite your **Quickwrite**, Part I, using at least two of the expressions you just learned.
3. Work in small groups. Use the following chart to share as much as you know about the meanings and purposes of various celebrations. First, call out and list as many celebrations as you can think of. Choose five from the list and complete the chart.

CELEBRATIONS

Name of Celebration

1. ____________ 2. ____________ 3. ____________ 4. ____________ 5. ____________

____________ ____________ ____________ ____________ ____________

Purpose of Celebration

1. ____________ 2. ____________ 3. ____________ 4. ____________ 5. ____________

____________ ____________ ____________ ____________ ____________

Activities Associated with Celebration

1. ____________ 2. ____________ 3. ____________ 4. ____________ 5. ____________

____________ ____________ ____________ ____________ ____________

What do these activities symbolize?

1. ____________ 2. ____________ 3. ____________ 4. ____________ 5. ____________

____________ ____________ ____________ ____________ ____________

Food Associated with Celebration

1. ____________ 2. ____________ 3. ____________ 4. ____________ 5. ____________

____________ ____________ ____________ ____________ ____________

What do these foods symbolize?

1. ____________ 2. ____________ 3. ____________ 4. ____________ 5. ____________

____________ ____________ ____________ ____________ ____________

Clothing Associated with the Celebration

1. ____________ 2. ____________ 3. ____________ 4. ____________ 5. ____________

____________ ____________ ____________ ____________ ____________

What does this clothing symbolize?

1. ____________ 2. ____________ 3. ____________ 4. ____________ 5. ____________

____________ ____________ ____________ ____________ ____________

Decorations Associated with the Celebration

1. ____________ 2. ____________ 3. ____________ 4. ____________ 5. ____________

____________ ____________ ____________ ____________ ____________

What do they symbolize?

1. ____________ 2. ____________ 3. ____________ 4. ____________ 5. ____________

____________ ____________ ____________ ____________ ____________

CELEBRATIONS

Other Things Associated with the Celebration

1. ____________ 2. ____________ 3. ____________ 4. ____________ 5. ____________

____________ ____________ ____________ ____________ ____________

What do they symbolize?

1. ____________ 2. ____________ 3. ____________ 4. ____________ 5. ____________

____________ ____________ ____________ ____________ ____________

Read, Discuss, and Describe and Explain a Celebration

A. READ ABOUT IT

Chinese New Year is one of the most important holidays in Chinese culture. People celebrate it in Taiwan, mainland China, and in cities around the world that have large Chinese populations, such as San Francisco and New York City. The following article, "A Chinese New Year Celebration," was written by Joyce Jue, the author of several Chinese cookbooks. In the article, Jue emphasizes the importance of food in the Chinese New Year celebration.

LEARNING STRATEGY

Forming Concepts: Guessing instead of stopping and looking up new words increases your reading speed and your comprehension.

As you read, do not worry if you do not understand all of the words; just try to guess their meanings. We have given explanations of some of the most difficult ones in the margin.

Threads

Many places around the world have large celebrations in February: Fasching in Germany and Switzerland, Mardi Gras in New Orleans, and Carnival in Brazil.

- Before you read, share your knowledge of the following kinds of parties with your classmates:

  an open house   a buffet   a banquet   afternoon tea

  Now, share your knowledge of these Chinese food items. Have you ever eaten any of these?

  dumplings   spring rolls   pudding cakes
  sesame balls   winter melon soup   bird's nest soup

- As you read, try to answer this question:

  What is the main purpose of Chinese New Year?

A CHINESE NEW YEAR CELEBRATION

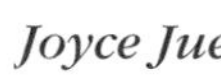

Joyce Jue

1 As my non-Chinese husband, Randy, quickly realized, Chinese New Year is a time for enormous family get-togethers that revolve around food. His first taste of Chinese New Year, one February day just after we'd met ten years ago, was a delicious culture shock. At first he was overwhelmed by the size of my family—30 to 40 aunts and uncles, cousins, nephews and nieces, plus close family friends—all assembled for an open house with a buffet. But his shock was softened by the array of brilliant food and fine spirits carefully prepared for all the banquets, dinner parties, afternoon teas and open houses that make up the New Year celebration. Today, Randy's an expert on Chinese New Year, and one of its biggest celebrants!

2 New Year is based in the Chinese *lunar* calendar and marks the first day of spring. The festivities last for two weeks. It's a time of renewal: We traditionally spend the days prior to New Year in feverish activity that will promote a more promising year. It's an exhilarating time: We thoroughly clean and sweep the house, have our hair cut and washed, pay *debts* in full and settle all family quarrels—all to start fresh. It's a time to shop for new clothes, fresh food, fruits and gifts, and to stop at the bank for crisp new bills to stuff into red "lucky money" envelopes that we give to children. These activities cleanse the soul and repel evil spirits and misfortune. They ensure a year of prosperity, success and good luck.

lunar: having to do with the moon

debts: money owed

3 At New Year, we expect friends and relatives to drop in any time for tea and snacks. Randy likes to visit the aunts who make the best dumplings and hot appetizers. Auntie Linda is the most traditional in my family: She treats us to her crisp spring rolls, sweet pan-fried pudding cakes, sticky sesame balls and steamed and crisp dumplings.

4 Not all the food set out for New Year is to be eaten—by now, Randy knows not to touch the gorgeous oranges, colossal *pomelos,* juicy peaches and fragrant tangerines stacked pyramid-style on flat plates that are displayed throughout the house. We put the fruit plates in special places around the house—on the mantel near an *altar,* on a shelf in the kitchen, on dressers on the bedroom—for good luck and longevity. And we won't eat this fruit until after the celebrations are over.

pomelos: a large yellow fruit, similar to a grapefruit

altar: a table on which people offer things to their god(s) or ancestors

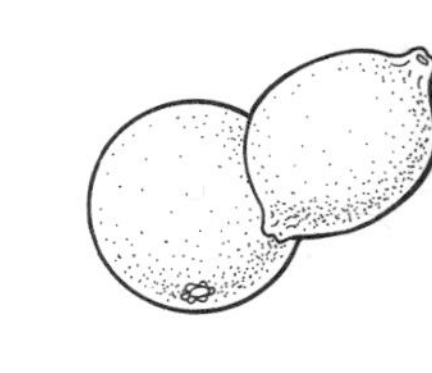

5 At the end of New Year's Day, the New Year feast is set out. My mom's New Year dinner is usually an array of traditional, symbolic dishes, plus an assortment of family favorites. There is always a banquet-style soup—perhaps steamed whole winter melon soup served in its hollowed-out shell, or a lovely bird's nest soup floating in a delicate broth. Out of respect for religion, we also have *jai,* a Buddhist vegetarian dish. To emphasize abundance and wealth, we set out a succulent poached chicken, chopped into bite-sized pieces and served with a green onion-and-ginger dip, and a whole fish shimmering in a delicate sauce.

6 It's a dinner not to be missed.

B. WHAT DO YOU REMEMBER?

In small groups, answer these questions about "A Chinese New Year Celebration."

1. What is the main purpose of Chinese New Year?
2. If you were celebrating Chinese New Year, which of the following would you most likely do? Check the correct statements.

_________ Decorate the house with bowls of fruit

_________ Have your hair cut

_________ Start arguments with family members

_________ Clean the house

_________ Buy new clothes

_________ When friends drop in, you tell them to go away.

Threads

Ralph & Patsy Martin of Quartzsite, Arizona have married each other 51 times.

Now, look at the activities you did not check. Make them correct for Chinese New Year by changing some of the words in the statements.

3. Match the New Year activities and foods Jue discusses with their meanings. There may be more than one answer for some activities.

MEANINGS		ACTIVITIES
a. Repel evil spirits and misfortune	_____	Eat poached chicken
b. Bring prosperity and good luck	_____	Decorate with fruit
c. Ensure longevity	_____	Eat *jai*
d. Show respect for religion	_____	Clean the house
e. Emphasize abundance	_____	Give money envelopes to children

LEARNING STRATEGY

Managing Your Learning: Looking at how other writers organize their ideas helps you organize your own writing assignment.

C. WRITING CONVENTIONS: ORGANIZING IDEAS

Notice these writing conventions in Joyce Jue's article:

1. Make a simple outline of Joyce Jue's article. First, list the purpose of each paragraph in the article. Then, list the ideas or examples in each paragraph (except for the conclusion). We have started the outline for you, so fill in the missing information:

I. Purpose: Introduction
Ideas/Examples:

II. Purpose: Give background
Ideas/Examples:

III. Purpose: Give some information about food

IV. Purpose: Explain decorations
Ideas/Examples:

V. Purpose: Explain main activity (banquet) in detail
Ideas/Examples:

VI. Purpose: To conclude

2. What tense does Jue use throughout the article? Why?
3. Review Paragraph 4.

a. Find the adjectives the author uses with each of the following:

________________	oranges	______________	pomelos
________________	peaches	______________	tangerines

b. Draw a picture of the fruit plates. How do you know what they look like? What expression does Jue use to describe them?

4. Circle the words and expressions Jue uses to explain the meaning and purpose of Chinese New Year, New Year food, and activities.

Threads

Roasted Camel, a traditional Bedouin wedding dish, is eggs, stuffed into fish, stuffed into chickens, stuffed into sheep, stuffed into a whole camel.

SUMMARY

- A good way to organize information in an article about a celebration is similar to the way Joyce Jue did it. (Each roman numeral indicates a paragraph.)

I. Introduction: State the purpose of the holiday and/or main activities
II. Body: Give background on the holiday or the history and traditional activities for the holiday
III. Body: Write about decorations and their meanings
IV. Body: Write about foods and their meanings
V. Conclusion

The body paragraphs of the article should include information on activities, food, and decorations associated with the celebration, along with their meaning. (It does not really matter what order you present these paragraphs in, as long as each one has only one main purpose.)

- Use the present tense when you describe a celebration; you are talking about what people *traditionally* do—what they do every time they have a particular celebration.
- Jue uses good descriptive words and phrases: "gorgeous oranges," "colossal pomelos," tangerines "stacked, pyramid style." When you use descriptive language in an article about food and decorations, people can really see and almost taste what you are describing.
- Jue uses a lot of the expressions for explaining purpose and meaning that you saw in Part II: "To emphasize abundance and wealth, we . . ." Make sure you use expressions like these when you discuss a celebration.

PRACTICE WRITING

Use your ideas from your **Quickwrite** in Part I to write a new paragraph on a holiday or celebration. Make sure you include the following:

- the habitual present tense
- descriptive words and phrases
- purpose and meaning expressions

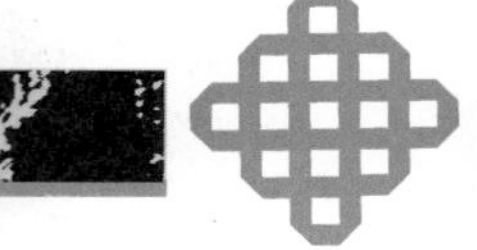

PART III

Gather Information and Describe and Explain a Celebration

A. PLAN AND ORGANIZE

Choose a celebration you would like to write about. It can be one that you are familiar with, or one that is new to you. It can be from your country or culture, or another country or culture. If you choose a celebration that is new to you, gather as much information about it as possible. Interview someone at school and/or go to the library and find books and articles about it.

Even if the celebration is familiar to you, start your work by answering as many of these questions as you can:

I. What is the name of the celebration?
What do people usually/traditionally do for this celebration?
What events occur: In what order?
Activities? Rituals? Games?
Music? Dances?
Give presents? Meals?

II. What is the celebration's background?
What is its history?
What is it for?
Does it change anything? (that is, does it create a change in someone's life?)

For example, a marriage ceremony joins two people)
What does it mean? (for example, Chinese New Year means "renewal" or "spring is here," etc.)

III. What foods, drinks, or meals traditionally go with the celebration?
Do they symbolize anything? What?
Do they have a function? (for example, to bring luck?)

IV. Do people wear special clothing for the celebration?
What does the clothing symbolize?

V. Are there special decorations for the celebration?
What do they symbolize? (for example, the evergreen Christmas tree symbolizes life in the dead of winter.)

B. SHARE

Bring your notes to class. In small groups, take turns telling about the celebration you have chosen. Be prepared to give lots of examples.

C. PREPARE

Write a short description of one aspect of the celebration. You can choose food and its meaning, clothing and its meaning, activities, etc.

When you finish, exchange your paper with a classmate. Read and make suggestions. Then, rewrite any parts you feel you can improve. You can use this paragraph later in the body of your assignment.

D. WRITE!

Now you are ready to write. Choose one of the following topics. As you write, keep in mind the goals you set in previous chapters.

1. Write about a celebration from your native country or culture. Explain the purpose of the celebration, and include at least two of the following:

- activities associated with it and what they symbolize
- history of the celebration
- special food and what it symbolizes
- special clothes and what they symbolize
- decorations and what they symbolize

After completing assignment 1, try the following for further practice:

2. Explain and give examples of the quotation at the beginning of the chapter:

We eat whenever life becomes dramatic: at weddings, birthdays, funerals, at parting and at welcoming home, or at any moment which a group decides is worthy of remark.

—Margaret Visser, from *The Rituals of Dinner*

3. Research: Find out about a celebration in another culture or country. Describe and explain it. Compare it to a similar one in your country or culture, too, if you want.

4. Combine ideas from a previous chapter with ideas from this chapter. For example, describe a celebration that has to do with naming (Chapter 3), or one that is associated with a special place (Chapter 5); or write about a song that has to do with a celebration (Chapter 6).

Assess

A. REFLECT

On the Reflections on My Writing chart (see Appendix A), fill in the boxes for Chapter 7.

B. EXCHANGE

Exchange your paper with a classmate and answer these questions:

1. What is your partner's first paragraph about? Does it clearly explain the purpose of the celebration?
2. What are the body paragraphs about?

   1st body paragraph: ______________________________

   2nd body paragraph: ______________________________

   3rd body paragraph: ______________________________
3. List some descriptive words and expressions your partner has used. Are they good choices? Do you have any suggestions for improvement?
4. Has your partner adequately explained the meaning and purpose of the celebration? What words and expressions has he or she used?

Threads

Years in the Chinese calendar:
1993—Rooster
1994—Dog
1995—Pig
1996—Rat
1997—Ox

C. REWRITE

Rewrite your paper, or just the parts that your partner or teacher found to be incomplete or unclear. As you write, consider the answers to the questions in Exercise B, or any other recommendations your partner had. Also, check to see that you have improved the area(s) you wanted to work on at the end of Chapter 6 (see Chapter 6, page 76).

D. LOOK AHEAD

Now, write **one thing** you would like to improve in the next writing assignment:

I'm going to work on. . .

____

____

____

CHAPTER 8

Favorite Movies

Good movies make you care, make you believe in possibilities again.

—Pauline Kael,
American movie critic

Art reflects the people who create and enjoy it. As a kind of art, movies say a lot about who we are and how we view ourselves. In fact, we can learn a lot about ourselves and our culture by analyzing movies and expressing our opinions about them. In this chapter, you are going to talk about movies and express your opinions about them.

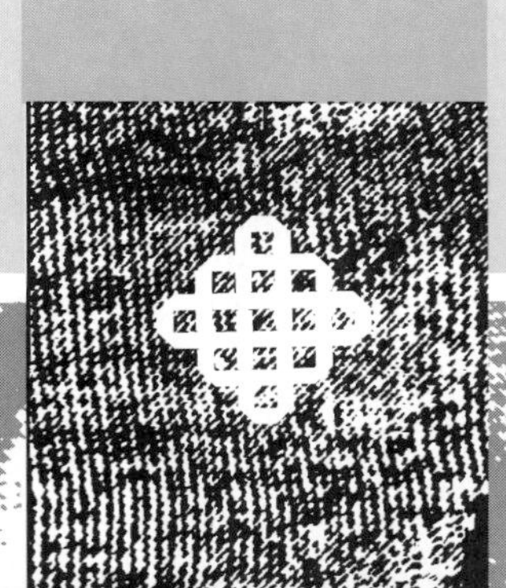

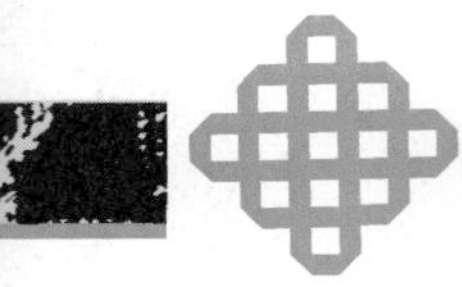

PART I

Get Started

A. TAKE A LOOK

Look at the following pictures. They are **movie stills,** photographs from movies. In small groups, try to guess the names of the movies, or the types of movies they are (comedy, adventure, etc.).

a. ____________________

b. ____________________

c. ____________________

d. ____________________

LEARNING STRATEGY

Managing Your Learning: Focussing on specific information is one way of centering your learning and improving comprehension.

B. LISTEN AND MATCH

Now, listen to four conversations about the movies in Exercise A. Try to match the conversation with the movie each speaker is talking about. Write the number of the conversation next to the picture it goes with. Listen as many times as you want.

C. REMEMBER

Now listen again. This time, answer these questions about the conversations in small groups.

1. What two things does Judy like about *The Wizard of Oz*?
2. What does Sam like about the movies *E.T*?
3. What does Joy love about *Gone With the Wind*?
4. What two things does Mike like about *Lawrence of Arabia*?

Interview

A. BRAINSTORM

How much do you already know about the movies? Work in small groups. Write examples of movie types, titles, actors, and reasons to like movies in the following chart. Write as many as you can.

TYPES OF MOVIES	*MOVIE TITLES*
Example: **comedy**	Example: ***The Gold Rush***

FAMOUS ACTORS/ACTRESSES	*REASONS PEOPLE LIKE MOVIES*
Example: **Charlie Chaplin**	Example: **good acting**

B. DISCUSS

Now, ask your partner questions about his or her favorite movies. Use ideas from Exercise A.

Examples:

1. What's your favorite movie?
2. What did you like about it?
3. Who is your favorite actress? Actor? Why?
4. What's your favorite kind of movie?
5. What movies have you seen recently? What did you think of them?

Now, think of your own questions to ask about movies.

Quickwrite

LEARNING STRATEGY

Personalizing: Writing about whatever *you* want helps make you a more fluent writer.

Write about *your* favorite movie. Write for ten minutes without stopping. Do not worry about grammar or spelling; just get your ideas on paper.

Threads

American actress Lillian Gish made her first movie in 1912 and her last movie in 1987.

Language Expansion

A. WORD LIST

Following are words and expressions people use to talk about movies.

LEARNING STRATEGY

Forming Concepts: Guessing the meanings of new words can help make you a more confident learner with greater comprehension ability.

How many do you already know? In small groups, share the definitions you know. If you are not sure of a word, guess.

Give examples of each starred (*) word.

SUPER WORD LIST 8: MOVIES

movie still	theme music	cinematography	to act
classic movie*	special effects	scene	to direct
dialogue	performance	location	
script	actor,* actress		
the (amount or type of) violence	director*		

B. EXPRESSING YOUR OPINION

When you express your opinion about a movie, you say whether or not you liked it, and why. Here are two examples:

- I liked *Gone With the Wind* because the acting is great.
- I didn't like *Gone With the Wind* because the story is unrealistic.

You have already listed reasons people like or dislike movies (**Interview**, Part I). Now, think of adjectives to describe movies.

LEARNING STRATEGY

Managing Your Learning: When you work with others, you can learn from them.

1. Work in small groups. Fill in the chart. Take turns. Fill in as many blanks as you can, then pass the chart to your neighbor.

LIST A: **Names of Movies You Have Seen**	LIST B: **Thing to Have an Opinion about**	LIST C: **Adjectives**
Gone With the Wind	the acting	boring
The Wizard of Oz	the story	good/bad
E.T.	the location	
The Terminator	the theme music	
	the dialogue	
	the amount of violence	

LEARNING STRATEGY

Remembering New Material: Using new words in sentences that are meaningful to you helps you remember them.

2. Now, take turns expressing your opinion. Use ideas from the lists in Item 1.

Example: I didn't like/I liked <u>Batman</u> (List A) because the <u>costumes</u> (List B) is/are <u>great</u> (List C).

Read, Discuss, and Express Your Opinion

A. READ ABOUT IT

Movie **critics** (or **reviewers**) write about new movies in newspapers and magazines. They usually say whether or not they liked the movie, and why. This helps people decide if they want to see the movie. Read this movie review of *Star Trek VI: The Undiscovered Country,* from *USA Today.* Do not worry if you do not understand all the words; just try to guess their meanings. We have given explanations of the most difficult ones in the margin.

- Before you read, share everything you already know about the "Star Trek" TV show and movies with the class.

LEARNING STRATEGY

Managing Your Learning: Having a specific question in mind as you read helps you understand what you are reading.

- As you read, try to answer this question:

Does the reviewer like *Star Trek VI*? Try to find a sentence that says whether or not she likes the movie.

'TREK VI' SETS SAIL ON A NEW MISSION (Movie Review)

Susan Wloszczyna

1 There are plenty of reasons to like *Star Trek VI: The Undiscovered Country,* supposedly the last movie the old TV cast will make.

2 For one thing, it's funny. The fact that most of the actors in the series are approaching old age is a running joke—Bones (DeForest Kelley) *sets the tone* early in the film as he jokingly wonders about a surprise meeting of the Federation of Planets: "Maybe they're *throwing* us a retirement party."

sets the tone: ***creates a feeling***
throwing: ***giving***

he looks fat
he's wearing a wig (false hair)
energetic

3 There's no use denying the Enterprise crew is showing its 25 years: James Coohan's Scotty seems to be *hiding a meteor under his shirt;* William Shatner's Capt. Kirk looks as if *a cat is napping on his head;* even Leonard Nimoy's Spock ears aren't quite as *perky.* But there's still life in the graying warriors, even after their last movie adventure, *Star Trek V,* which wasn't very successful.

dead
someone who is attractive to women/a Star Trek fan

4 Director Nicholas Meyer gets almost everything right—he pays respect to *late* Star Trek creator Gene Roddenberry and jokes about Captain Kirk's reputation as an outer space *Casanova.*

5 And you don't have to be a *Trekkie* to enjoy the time plot. Reflecting the United States' uneasy alliance with the former Soviet Union, the Star Trek crew tries to be friendly with its former enemy, the Klingons. Our heroes don't like the peace policy much though, considering the Klingons killed Kirk's son. Because the captain finds it difficult to hide his distrust of the Klingons, he becomes a prime suspect when some assassins attack the Klingon leaders.

a TV channel that shows only U.S. congressional hearings; in other words, boring
dream-like

6 The dialog was one thing I didn't like about the movie. It sounds like an intergalactic *C-SPAN.* And the effects are just ordinary. (The most dazzling is the attack on the Klingons, with fuchsia blood spilling out in *surrealistic* blobs.)

7 Of course, *Star Trek* was never about special effects, but about relationships—both among its crew members and with its audience. *Star Trek VI* more than upholds this tradition, making it a satisfying finale for our heroes' adventures.

B. WHAT DO YOU REMEMBER?

In small groups, answer these questions about the review of *Star Trek VI.*

1. Does the reviewer like the movie? How do you know? Find some words and expressions that the writer uses to express her opinion.
2. Check things about the movie the reviewer discusses:

		OPINION
_____	the effects	______________________
_____	the actors	______________________
_____	the music	______________________
_____	the director	______________________
_____	the (amount or type of) violence	______________________
_____	the plot or the story	______________________
_____	the dialog	______________________
_____	the location	______________________
_____	the costumes	______________________
_____	the music	______________________

3. Now give the reviewer's opinion of each of the things you checked in Item 2. Use your own words.

4. This review is **humorous** (funny). The humor makes the review a little difficult to understand. With a partner, pick out three humorous statements and restate them in your own words. (Hint: Look for descriptions of the actors.)

HUMOROUS STATEMENT	WHAT IT REALLY MEANS
Example: ". . . It [the dialogue] sounds like an intergalactic C-SPAN."	The dialogue is boring
a. ______________________________	a. ______________________________
b. ______________________________	b. ______________________________
c. ______________________________	c. ______________________________

5. Does this review make you want to see the movie? Why? Why not?

C. WRITING CONVENTIONS: A MOVIE REVIEW

Answer these questions about the writing conventions in the review of *Star Trek VI.*

1. Where does the reviewer state her opinion about the movie? Is it clear?
2. What verb tense does the reviewer use? Give five examples from the review.

____

____

____

____

____

3. What does the movie title look like in the article? (How is it typed?)
4. The reviewer tells you who plays each character. She does this two ways. What are they?

First Way: ______________________________________

Second Way: ____________________________________

5. Does the reviewer quote any dialogue from the movie? How does she do this?

SUMMARY

- You should state your opinion of the movie clearly and early in the review.
- You should use the present tense when you write about a movie.

- You must *italicize* (or *underline*) the movie title.
- If you are going to talk about the actors in the movie, it is a good idea to say which characters they play. There are two ways you can do this:

  —Use parentheses: **Bones (DeForest Kelley)** sets the tone . . .
  —Use the possessive: **William Shatner's Capt. Kirk** looks as if . . .

- It is a good idea to quote lines from a movie. Whenever you use quotes, you can use a comma or a colon to separate the quote from the person who said it. You **must** use quotation marks around the quote.

PRACTICE WRITING

Use your ideas from **Quickwrite** in Part I to write a new paragraph on your favorite movie. As you write, make sure you include the following:

- the title
- one or two characters and the names of the actors who play them
- some dialogue (in the form of a quote)

Also, make sure you use the present tense.

PART III

Gather Information and Express Your Opinion

A. PLAN AND ORGANIZE

With the class, make a list of movies to see and review. You can either go to a movie theater or rent a video. Look at current newspapers and magazines for ideas.

For each movie on the list ask:

- Who in the class has already seen it?
- If you have not seen it, what have you already heard or read about it?

See the movie with a partner. Take notes or be prepared to take notes immediately afterwards. (Hint: If you rent a movie, you can stop and rewind it to see important or difficult parts over again. You also have more light to take notes, and can talk to your partner without bothering anybody.)

B. SHARE

Back in class, work in small groups. Discuss the film you saw with your group. As you discuss your film, summarize it and express your opinion about it.

Now, find your partner or someone who saw the same movie as you. Fill in the Part A of the following chart together. Then, fill in Part B by yourself.

Part A.

Title of Movie: ______________________________

____

Plot: (List of Main Points): ______________________________

____

____

____

Part B.

Overall Opinion: ______________________________

____

____

Reasons for Your Opinion: (the acting, the dialogue, etc.)

____

____

Restatement of Opinion: (Note: Say it in different words.)

____

____

Threads

Most popular films in different countries in 1990: Hong Kong-*All for the Winner* Iran-*Courtship* Mexico-La *risa en vacaciones* Taiwan-*God of Gamblers* Brazil-*Cinema Paradiso*

C. PREPARE

After you fill in the chart, write a one paragraph summary of the plot of the movie. Do this alone. Then, compare your summary with your partner's. Did you leave anything out? Rewrite it if you think you can make it better.

After you write your summary paragraph, write a paragraph expressing your opinion of the movie you saw. Try to write at least five sentences. Say *why* you liked or did not like the movie, and explain your reason. Give examples and make a conclusion.

Threads

In 1991, *Terminator 2: Judgment Day* made $204.3 million.

D. WRITE!

Now you are ready to write. Choose one of the following topics. As you write, keep in mind the goals you set in previous chapter.

1. Summarize and express your opinion of the movie you saw. Use the chart you made in Exercise D.
2. Write about your favorite classic (old) movie. Summarize it and express your opinion.

After completing assignments 1 and 2, try the following for further practice:

3. Write about the most popular foreign film in your country last year. By "foreign film", we mean any film that was not made in your native country. Explain why you think it was popular.
4. Write about the quote about movies at the beginning of the chapter. What do you think it means? Do you agree or disagree?

Good movies make you care, make you believe in possibilities again.
—Pauline Kael, American movie critic

5. Combine ideas from a previous chapter with ideas from this chapter. For example, write about a movie that deals with the learning process (Chapter 4), special places (Chapter 5), music or musicians (Chapter 6), or celebrations (Chapter 7).

Assess

A. REFLECT

On the Reflections on My Writing chart (see Appendix A), fill in the boxes for Chapter 8: Movies.

B. EXCHANGE

Exchange your paper with a classmate and answer these questions:

1. Is the plot summary clear?
2. Does your partner clearly state his or her opinion of the movie? Does your partner given an example? Does he or she have a conclusion?

C. REWRITE

Rewrite your paper, or just the parts that your partner or teacher found to be incomplete or unclear. As you write, consider the answers to the questions in Exercise B, or any other recommendations your partner had. Also, check to see that you have improved the area(s) you wanted to work on at the end of Chapter 7 (see Chapter 7, page 90).

D. LOOK AHEAD

Now, write **one thing** you would like to improve in the next writing assignment:

I'm going to work on. . .

____

____

____

9 CHAPTER

Future Gadgets

Necessity is the mother of invention.
—Jonathan Swift, 18th century Irish-born
English writer

The things that we invent often reflect our hopes and fears. Many modern inventions express our desire for an easier, safer, or faster life. And technology advances so quickly that recent inventions soon become obsolete. What will people invent for tomorrow? And what will these inventions say about the people of tomorrow? In this chapter, you are going to predict and write about an invention of the future.

PART I

Get Started

A. TAKE A LOOK

Look at these illustrations of technological devices. Try to identify each one.

LEARNING STRATEGY

Forming Concepts: Use experience from the past to make intelligent guesses and to concentrate on the material.

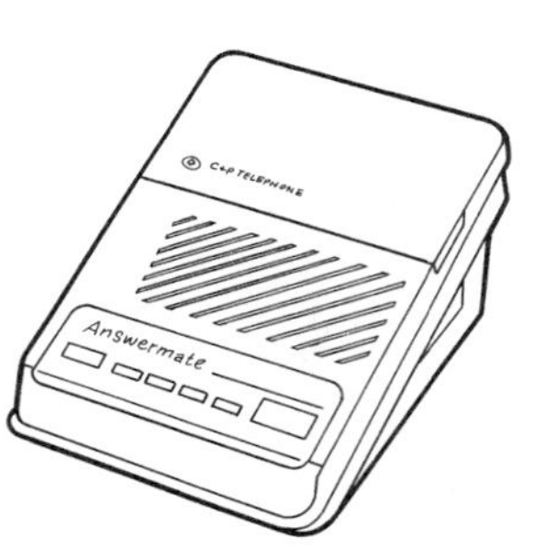

a. ______________________  b. ______________________ c. ______________________

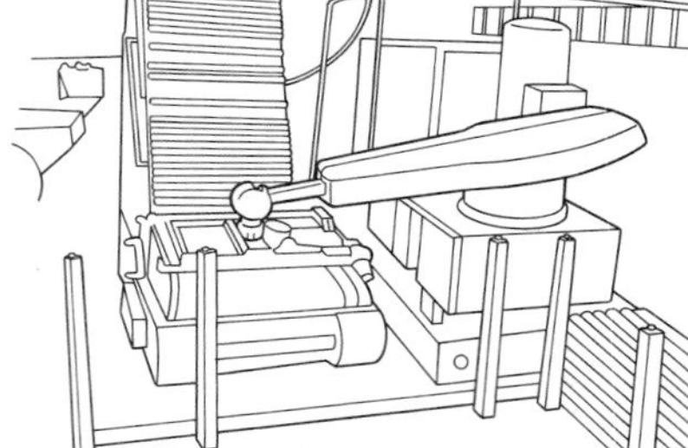

d. ______________________ e. ______________________ f. ______________________

B. GUESS

Listen to a classmate describe a future gadget. The student will describe it without saying what it is. He or she can say things like:

- what it is like
- what it looks like
- how it works

Your group will try to guess the object.

C. DISCUSS

Still in your groups, talk about the objects in Exercise A.

1. Which of these have you ever used?
2. Which of these do you own?
3. What is your opinion of each device? Is it useful? Does it make life easier or harder? Explain your answers.

Interview

LEARNING STRATEGY

Forming Concepts: Using your imagination freely will help you become a more fluent thinker and writer.

A. BRAINSTORM

As a class, brainstorm for technological devices that are commonplace today, but did not exist when you were a child. Then, make a list of any devices you have heard or read about that are being developed now, and will someday be a part of everyday life. If you can not think of any, guess, or use your imagination. What do you *think* is possible in the near future?

Technological devices that did not exist when I was a child:
For example: fax machines VCRs

Technological devices of tomorrow:
For example: video phones

Work in small groups. You and your group are going to create a device that will allow people to do something they cannot do now. Talk about

- what you will create
- how it will work
- why people will want to buy it
- possible problems the device may create
- etc.

B. DISCUSS

Now, ask a classmate questions about technological devices in his or her everyday life:

1. What technological devices do you use in your everyday life?
2. How do they work?
3. How do they make your life better?
4. What doesn't exist yet, but you think would be a good idea?

Quickwrite

Write about one technological device that is an important part of your life. Write for ten minutes without stopping. Do not worry about grammar or spelling; just get your ideas on paper.

PART II

Language Expansion

A. WORD LIST

Following are words and expressions people use to talk about technological devices. How many do you already know? In small groups, share the meanings you know.

Give examples of the starred (*) words.

SUPER WORD LIST 9: GADGETS

gadget*	complex*	to invent,
product*	simple*	to work
innovation	technological	to develop
process	innovative	to simplify
research, researcher*		to operate*
invention*		to come up with*
technology		
	on the market	

B. *BY* + GERUND

One way to talk about how something works is to use *works by* + *Ving:*

• (the object) *works* / *operates* *by* Verb + *ing*

For example:
The electric garage door opener *works* simply by pushing a button.
Cellular phones *work* by having a transmitter placed every few miles.

1. Write five sentences explaining how the objects in Exercise A, **Get Started**, work. Use X *works* by V+*ing*
2. Rewrite your **Quickwrite** assignment, using at least one X *works* by Verb+*ing*.

C. *WILL + VERB*

If you want to make predictions about objects that will soon be available, just use *will* + Verb.
For example:
Sony *will* probably be developing smaller and smaller CD players.

Threads

Americans spent $1.38 million on cellular telephones in 1991.

Electronic Industries Association

D. PRACTICE

It's 1970. Pick three things in Exercise A, **Get Started**, that have not been invented yet. Write a prediction about each one, using *will* + Verb.

Read, Discuss, and Predict Future Technology

A. READ ABOUT IT

You often find stories about technological innovations in business and science magazines, and in the business and science sections of daily

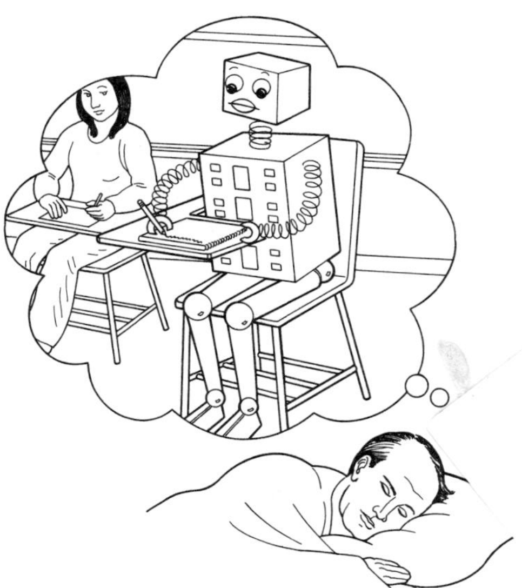

newspapers. These articles are both informative and entertaining; they make us aware of new products that are or will soon be available.

Read the following article "Essential Futuristic Gadgets," which first appeared in a newspaper in January, 1992. Don't worry if you do not understand all of the words; just try to guess. We have given explanations of the most difficult ones in the margin.

LEARNING STRATEGIES

Managing Your Learning: Prepare for reading the article by reviewing material you already know.

- Before you read, review the list of technological devices of tomorrow that you made on page 106, Part I. Then, answer these questions:

1. What are cellular phones? How do they work?
2. What are portable computers? How do they work?
3. What is a fax machine? How does it work?
4. What are the different kinds of personal computer printers? How do they work?
5. What is a compact disc (a CD)? Digital Audio Tape (DAT)? How do they work?

- As you read, think about this question:
  Is the article about fantastic products that we may never see or is it about realistic inventions that will soon be on the market?

ESSENTIAL FUTURISTIC GADGETS

by Tim Jackson

1 It may be bad news for competitors, but it's terrific news for us: A whole range of *innovative* products will soon be available. Most of these products are not fantastic technological innovations, but interesting combinations of existing technologies.

new and better

2 Here are some new gadgets that, though you may not think so now, may be yours within the next year.

3 • **The wrist-watch telephone**. Today's mobile phones work by having a transmitter placed every few miles. When your portable phone gets too far away from one transmitter area, or "cell", a computer tells it to change to another one. Because cells are currently rather large, portable phones have to be large, and therefore, expensive.

4 Japan's telephone company, NTT, now has a cellular phone that works with much smaller cells. The disadvantage is that thousands more transmitters will be needed; the advantage is that the phones don't have to be as powerful as before, so they'll cost less. They're already available in Tokyo, and they weigh less than 20 grams—just the right size to go on your wrist!

5 • **Flat TV screens.** The most recent computer innovation was the note-book sized computer, that weighed five or six pounds. The manufacturer said it could do everything a personal computer could do, but in fact, it was not quite powerful enough to do the work of a typical personal computer.

6 Since 1991, however, Toshiba has been operating a *joint venture* with IBM to make high-quality, full-color, flat television screens. They use less power than regular TV screens, and can be used with portable computers. They can do things that even the most complex personal computers can do, such as computer-aided design.

an agreement to work together

7 • **Color faxes.** The latest fax machines can send a one-page letter in four seconds instead of a minute, with higher-quality copying than ever before—but only in black and white. Now, researchers at NTT have developed new, smaller faxes that work quickly and more cheaply, and in color. The process is called *ion flow.* Ion flow allows an image to be recorded on paper directly, and then developed as in a photocopy machine. It can send a good color copy in three minutes.

8 • **The mini-compact disk.** Until recently, the people at Sony were trying to persuade the music world to use their Digital Audio Tape. These small cassettes provide the sound quality of a compact disk. Then Philips of Holland surprised its Japanese *rival* with a Digital Compact Cassette that works the same way. But a few weeks later Sony showed the world the Mini-Disc—a compact-disc machine with discs that are about one-forth the size of present-day CDs.

a company that's doing the same thing

9 Now Sony will probably be developing smaller and smaller CD players—(A wrist-watch player to go with your wrist-watch phone?) Most experts feel these mini-discs will be the *industry standard* for the next few years.

a model for other companies to follow

10 • **Domestic appliances**. Some new household appliances will be using a new technology called "fuzzy logic". Fuzzy log is a computer system that can make more than just "Yes" and "No" decisions; it can also make "Maybe" decisions. For example, Matsushita has come up with a vacuum cleaner that can sense how dirty your carpets are and then adjust its engine speed to match. Sharp has a Jacuzzi-style washing machine that speeds up the wash and makes a small amount of washing powder go further—simply by squirting jets of bubbles into the hot water as it *churns* backward and forward.

circulates

B. WHAT DO YOU REMEMBER?

In small groups, answer these questions about "Essential Futuristic Gadgets."

1. Are the products Jackson describes fantasies, or devices that will soon be common? How do you know?
2. Jackson says that all these devices are possible because of some current technology. Find the existing technology that made the futuristic gadget possible:

EXISTING TECHNOLOGY	FUTURISTIC GADGET
today's mobile phones	wrist-watch telephone
______________________	color fax
______________________	portable ink-jet printer
______________________	mini-compact disc
______________________	new household appliances

LEARNING STRATEGY

Personalizing: Putting new ideas into your own words helps you have a better understanding of them.

3. Now, explain in your own words how each futuristic gadget works, what it is for, or what is special about it.
4. Do you see possible problems with any of these new devices?
5. This article appeared at the beginning of 1992. Are any of the futuristic gadgets in the article common today?

C. WRITING CONVENTIONS: DESCRIBING AND PREDICTING FUTURE TECHNOLOGY

Answer these questions about the writing conventions in "Essential Futuristic Gadgets."

LEARNING STRATEGY

Managing Your Learning: Taking a look at how another writer has organized his or her ideas can help you become a better writer.

1. There is one sentence in the first paragraph that tells you the main idea of the article and even suggests how the reporter will organize his thoughts. Find that sentence and write it here:

____

____

2. In the body of the article, the reporter uses a special technique for listing all the items he is going to discuss. What is this technique?

____

Give an example.

____

3. What tense does the reporter use the most?

____

4. Many sentences use a particular verb form. Here is an example:

The disadvantage is that thousands more transmitters **will be needed**.

What do you call this verb form? Find three more examples in the article and write them here:

____

____

____

5. Describe how the information in the article is organized. For example, look at the bulleted items—the items with the dots in front of them. What information does the first paragraph (or the first few sentences) for each item contain? What information does the last paragraph (or sentences) contain? Is this style consistent throughout the whole article?

____

____

Threads

In 1990, U.S. companies spent $128.6 billion on advertising.

Newspaper Advertizing Bureau

SUMMARY

- In a technical article (as in a news article or an expository essay) you should state your main idea in the first paragraph. This prepares the readers, and gets their attention. Here you can also explain how you are going to organize your ideas.
- In technical, business, and news writing, you can use bullets (•) to list items you are going to talk about. This makes the readers' job easier; it emphasizes important items, and it helps the readers to skim and scan. However, a bulleted list must never contain chronological information (for example, action steps: "First you do this; then you do this", etc.)—this kind of information belongs in a numbered list (for example, 1., 2., etc.)

- This reporter mainly uses the present tense; this is because most of the gadgets have already been developed. Whenever he talks about something that is not here yet, he uses the future tense. (For example: Now Sony will probably be developing smaller and smaller CD players.)
- In the sentence, "The disadvantage is that thousands more transmitters will be needed," the verb is in the passive voice. You can use the passive voice when you write about technical subjects because the *agent* (the thing or person causing the action) often is **not important.** Review the formula:

  Object + *BE* + V*ed*
  OR: Object + *BE* + *Ving* + *by* + agent, when the agent is important.

  For example: The plutonium *will* be handled by a robot. (For more information on the passive voice, see Language Expansion, Chapter 3, page 30).
- This article has a consistent organizational pattern: a paragraph (or group of sentences) that gives background information follows each bulleted item. The next one or two paragraphs (or sentences) explain how the new device will work.

Threads

The first electronic computer (called ENIAC) was built at the University of Pennsylvania in 1943.

PRACTICE WRITING

Practice these conventions for writing a technical article. Take one or all of the items pictured in **Get Started,** Part I, and describe how it/they work. Make sure you include:

- an introduction that states your main idea
- a bulleted list (hint: you can use it to list parts)
- the passive voice (if appropriate)
- a logical organizational pattern that fits the topic

PART III

Gather Information and Predict Future Technology

A. ORGANIZE AND DEVELOP YOUR IDEAS

Get into small groups. Work as a team to develop a new technological device or product. The product does not have to be technical. For example, you can develop a new kind of toothpaste. Assign roles:

- One person can be a researcher, finding background information in science and business magazines in the library.
- One or two can be responsible for designing the object. Consider how it works and what it will be used for. You can also decide how it will be made, how big it will be, how much it will weigh, and how much it will cost.

- One person can be the artist. This person can draw the parts of the invention or product and how it will look when it is finished.

As a group, decide on a name for your product or invention.

B. SHARE

Now, present your invention to the class. Show the drawings. Ask and answer questions about each other's inventions.

C. PREPARE

Using input from your presentation, make any necessary changes to your product. Then, fill in the following chart with information about your invention:

What is it called?

____

____

What led to its discovery/invention? (Background)

____

____

What is it for?

____

____

How does it work?

____

____

What does it look like? (Size, weight. Is it similar to anything else?)

____

____

D. WRITE!

Now you are ready to write. Choose one of the following topics. As you write, keep in mind the goals you set in previous chapters.

1. Write about how the invention or product your group designed works. Include background information and any other information you developed with your group. You may add new information too, if you like.
2. Write about another group's product or invention. Include background information and any other information the group developed. You may add new information too, if you like.
3. Predict a technological gadget of future. Use *will* when you make predictions.

After completing assignments 1-3, try the following for further practice:

4. Explain what you think the quote at the beginning of this chapter means. Give examples to support your explanation.

   Necessity is the mother of invention.—Jonathan Swift

5. Combine ideas from a previous chapter with ideas from this chapter. For example, write about technical innovations in education and learning (Chapter 4), in the music industry (Chapter 6), or in movie-making (Chapter 8).

Assess

A. REFLECT

On the Reflections on My Writing chart (see Appendix A), fill in the boxes for Chapter 9: Future Gadgets.

Threads

When was it invented?
The Flush Toilet—1707
The Ball Point Pen—1938
The Zipper—1913

B. EXCHANGE

Exchange your paper with a classmate and answer these questions:

1. Does the first paragraph prepare you pretty well for the rest of the article?
2. Is the organization easy to follow?
3. Does the writer say what the object is called? Does he or she give background information on the device? Does he or she explain what it is for, how it works, or how it looks?

C. REWRITE

Rewrite your paper, or just the parts that your partner or teacher found to be incomplete or unclear. As you write, consider the answers to the questions in Exercise B, or any other recommendations your partner had. Also, check to see that you have improved the area(s) you wanted to work on at the end of Chapter 8 (see Chapter 8, page 102).

D. LOOK AHEAD

Now, write **one thing** you would like to improve in the next writing assignment:

I'm going to work on. . .

___

___

___

___

CHAPTER 10

Saving The Planet

The only thing that makes civilization go forward is the responsibility of individuals . . . for the species, for the culture, for the larger thing outside ourselves.

—Wallace Stegner, American writer

In this last chapter, we are going to look beyond ourselves to the planet Earth itself. What is our relationship with the natural world? Are we a part of nature, or apart from it? And what do our environmental problems reflect about us, all of us? In this chapter, you are going to think about environmental problems and propose solutions for them.

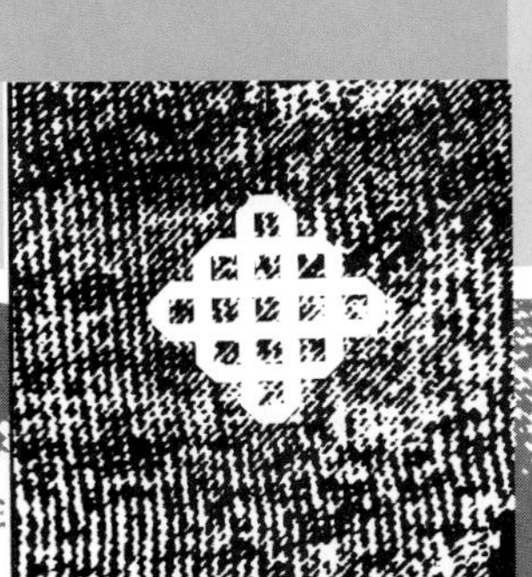

PART I

Get Started

A. TAKE A LOOK

Look at the following photographs. Work with a partner. Try to identify the problem shown in each photo. Write the name of the problem on the line beneath each one.

a. ____________________

b. ____________________

c. ____________________

d. ____________________

e. ____________________

f. ____________________

B. DISCUSS

The pictures in Exercise A all show environmental problems. What are the causes of these problems? In small groups, discuss and list the possible causes of the problems shown in the photos.

PROBLEM	POSSIBLE CAUSES
Water pollution	1. ____________________
	2. ____________________
	3. ____________________
Ozone hole	1. ____________________
	2. ____________________
	3. ____________________
Harm to wildlife	1. ____________________
	2. ____________________
	3. ____________________
Toxic waste	1. ____________________
	2. ____________________
	3. ____________________
Deforestation	1. ____________________
	2. ____________________
	3. ____________________
Garbage	1 ____________________
	2. ____________________
	3. ____________________

Share the information you discussed in your groups with the rest of the class. Then list any other environmental problems you can think of.

Interview

LEARNING STRATEGY

Understanding and Using Emotions: Listening to other people's thoughts and feelings helps you understand your own feelings.

Ask a partner the following questions about environmental problems, and then think of some of your own questions.

1. Which of the environmental problems you discussed in **Get Started** affect you personally? How?
2. Which of these problems affect your community? How?
3. In your opinion, are people doing enough to solve these problems?
4. Are you doing anything to solve these problems? What?

Now ask some of your own questions.

Quickwrite

Write about one environmental problem that you are interested in. You can describe it, explain why it is a problem, explain how it affects you personally, or propose a solution.

Write for ten minutes without stopping. Do not worry about grammar or spelling; just get your ideas on paper.

PART II

Language Expansion

A. WORD LIST

Following are words and expressions people use to talk about environmental problems. How many do you already know? In small groups, share the meanings you know.

Explain the starred (*) items in your own words.

SUPER WORD LIST 10: SAVING THE PLANET

issue	to engage in	short term profit*
deforestation*	to accomplish	
ozone depletion*	to commit (oneself) to	
species		
extinction*		
activism	obsolete	
(to take) direct action	endangered	
toxins		
pesticides		

B. MODALS

When you propose a solution to a problem, you should use words that make your point as strongly as possible. One way to do this is to use modals such as:

must *should* *ought to* *have to*

Look at these examples:

- More Americans *have* to start voting.
- People *should* engage in direct action in order to solve environmental problems.

LEARNING STRATEGY

Remembering New Material: Using new words in context helps increase your active vocabulary.

Look at the problems and causes chart you made in Part I. Take each problem and suggestion a solution for it. State your solution in one sentence using *have to, must, should,* and *ought to.*

PROBLEM	SOLUTION
Water pollution	________________
Ozone hole	________________
Harm to wildlife	________________
Toxic waste	________________
Deforestation	________________
Garbage	________________

C. SUFFIXES

In Chapter 4, you saw how learning about stems, prefixes, and suffixes can increase your vocabulary. In this chapter, you are going to take a closer look at suffixes and learn how they can change a stem's part of speech.

For example, take a look at how the noun *environment* changes when you add certain suffixes (word endings):

environment (noun) → environment**al** (adjective) → environment**ally** (adverb)

Examples:

- It's time to start thinking about ways to save the *environment*.
- We have many *environmental* problems right here in our own community.
- Let's hope the next election produces some *environmentally*-aware candidates.

LEARNING STRATEGY

Remembering New Material: Being able to recognize and use word endings helps you remember vocabulary.

As you can see, suffixes contain information about what the word means, as well as what part of speech the word is. Here are some common suffixes and their usual meanings:

SUFFIX	EXAMPLE	USUAL MEANING	PART OF SPEECH
-ment	environment	cause, means, result	noun
-al	environmental	having the qualities of	adjective
-ly	environmentally	in this manner	adverb
-ist	activist	one who is employed in (usually, a particular field)	noun
-ism	activism	action, state, condition	noun
-tion	deforestation	condition	noun
-able	profitable	capable of being	adjective
-ity	responsibility	the quality of or being an example of	noun
-ic	democratic	the quality or condition of	adjective
-ology	technology	science, the study of	noun

Practice using these words by rewriting your **Quickwrite** and including at least five of the words in the preceding chart.

D. CAUSE/RESULT STATEMENTS

Many times a solution to a problem involves getting other people to take action. You can often persuade people to take action by showing results with a cause/result statement. The cause part of the sentences includes the word *if,* and the result sometimes includes the word *then*.

Look at these examples:

- If we can't buy fruits and vegetables that have been grown without pesticides [CAUSE], then we'll have to start growing our own [RESULT].

Note: *Then* is optional (you don't have to use it).

- If it doesn't rain soon [CAUSE], we'll have to start rationing water [RESULT].
- If we don't do anything about the environment now [CAUSE], in ten years it will be too late [RESULT].

Note: You can reverse the order of the cause and result. For example:

- We'll have to start rationing water [RESULT] if it doesn't rain soon [CAUSE].

Notice that you do not use a comma when you reverse the order of the cause and result.

Threads

Endangered Species: Morrow Bay Kangaroo Rat (U.S.), Paradise Parrot (Australia), Snow Leopard (Asia)

IVCN Red List of Threatened Animals (1990)

Look at the following cause and result chart. Match the causes with the results. Note: There may be more than one result for each cause.

CAUSE If we . . .		RESULT
1. do not stop destroying the rain forest	a. _____	many animals we know today will disappear forever
2. continue to allow factories to leak toxins into the environment	b. _____	environmental problems will increase and our quality of life will worsen
3. continue to hunt endangered species	c. _____	many people may begin to have unexplained diseases
4. do not start voting for environmentally-aware political candidates	d. _____	there will be less oxygen in the atmosphere
5. continue to use pesticides	e. _____	there will be less drinkable water for humans and animals

Now, write complete cause/result sentences from the chart.

Example: If we continue to use pesticides, many people may begin to have unexplained diseases.

Read, Discuss, and Propose a Solution

A. READ ABOUT IT

The following article is based on an interview with Dr. Helen Caldicott. Dr. Caldicott is a physician from Australia. She is also an anti-nuclear activist. She co-founded the organization International Physicians for Social Responsibility. In this article, Dr. Caldicott talks about the environmental problems we face today, and what we can do about them. For further information on Dr. Caldicott's ideas, look for her book *If You Love This Planet.*

Read the following article. Do not worry if you do not understand all of the words; just try to guess. We have given explanations of the most difficult ones in the margin.

- Before you read, answer this question:

What is the most pressing environmental problem, in your opinion?

- As you read, think about this question:

Which of Dr. Caldicott's recommendations for saving the planet do you agree with?

SAVING THE PLANET

Dr. Helen Caldicott

immediate 1 People often ask me what I see as the single most *pressing*
environmental issue today. Actually, there is no single issue that is most
pressing. There are a number of them: overpopulation of one species,
disappearance which is us (homo sapiens); the *extinction* of thirty million other species;
deforestation; ozone depletion; greenhouse warming; chemical pollution;
and radioactive pollution. Those are just some of the issues—the main
ones—and they all have the same degree of seriousness. As a matter of fact,
if we don't do anything about any one of them, we're in serious trouble.

making sick 2 We've only ten years or less to reverse all the effects that are *ailing*
the planet, and if we don't start now, within ten years, it will be too late.
Nothing else really matters right now except saving life on the planet.

3 The primary question, of course, is what can we do about the state
of the environment? Some of the answers are working within the political
system and taking direct, individual action.

4 More Americans have to start voting. In Australia, we have always had
forced a *compulsory* system of voting. If we don't vote, we are fined $50. It works
extremely well. Everyone feels very proud that they vote and most people
know what issues they're voting about. I also suggest that independents run
tired of for Congress in the next election—I think many Americans are *fed up* with
the lack of choice that the two-party system offers.

5 The ideal situation would be to get people elected to Congress who
would only represent their political districts, not special interest groups
or their political party. These representatives come regularly to the
people who voted for them and say, "Look, we're going to vote on this
issue in Congress soon. How do you want *me* to vote?" That would be a
truly democratic system, and it would allow the introduction of new
political issues into the system, such as environmental concerns.

6 At this time, we have enough science, medical knowledge, and
money to save the planet in ten years. All we have to do is make a
political decision. That means we have to take control of our country
away from those who don't give a damn about what's happening to the
earth, those who only care about short term profit and loss. We have to
not useful anymore realize that that sort of thinking is *obsolete.*

7 Besides voting, direct action activism is another way to start saving
the planet. I think that people should engage in direct action as long as
there is no violence towards others; no one must be hurt. There are ways
to take direction action without violence—think of all that Gandhi
taking apart accomplished. For example, I'm not against *dismantling* bulldozers that
are going to knock over trees that house many species of birds and animals.

8 In fact, I spent many years trying to stop nuclear weapons production, and now we're starting to see some results. I started in 1978, so it took a little over ten years. Because we are now starting to see a decline in nuclear weapons production, I have great optimism. If we really commit ourselves to the task of saving the planet, we'll easily do it in ten years. We just need to stop sitting in our armchairs saying "What can I do?" We can do amazing things if we just decide to take action.

9 A specific problem that is going to affect all of us sooner or later is health problems caused by environmental pollution. Physicians are starting to notice diseases that seem to be caused by *toxins* in the environment—in the workplace and sometimes in the home. There are many toxins used in houses—insulating materials, the anti-stain chemicals that carpets are soaked in, and the glue that holds pressed-wood furniture together, just to name a few. Much of the food we eat contains pesticides, which are toxins. Doctors still don't know very much about the diseases caused by pesticides and household toxins. The average person doesn't really know what these chemicals are and what they do to the human body, but the chemical companies do. They do the tests on household toxins and pesticides, but the information rarely gets to the public. This is a new frontier of medicine that we have to go to work on very fast.

poisons

10 What I'm saying is that we should be aware of what we're exposing ourselves to and what we're putting in our bodies. We don't need pesticides or chemicals to grow excellent fruit. If we can't buy produce that has been grown without pesticides, we're going to have to start growing our own. As a matter of fact, growing our own produce not only allows us to stop poisoning ourselves, it also helps us get in touch with nature again. Ever since the industrial revolution, we have gradually lost touch with the soil, with plants, with nature—in effect, we've lost touch with ourselves, with our own souls. We're dying, and we're killing the earth as well. We must reverse this *trend* before it's too late.

way of doing things

Adapted from "Saving the Planet", in *Folio,* April 1992, KPFA Program Guide, pp. 1 and 26.

B. WHAT DO YOU REMEMBER?

In small groups, answer these questions about "Saving the Planet:"

1. Does Dr. Caldicott think one environmental issue that is more important than all the others?
2. What two general solutions does she propose for saving the earth?
3. In Dr. Caldicott's opinion, how should Congressional representatives serve the people who elected them?
4. Is Dr. Caldicott for or against direct action activism? What is her opinion of violent actions?
5. Is Dr. Caldicott for or against an action such as dismantling a bulldozer that is going to knock down trees?

LEARNING STRATEGY

Personalizing: When you paraphrase other people's ideas in your own words, you increase your understanding and your vocabulary.

6. Explain in your own words why Dr. Caldicott feels optimistic about the effect of direct action activism.
7. Who do *you* think Dr. Caldicott is referring to when she mentions people who only care about short term profit and loss?
8. What solution(s) does she propose for dealing with the problem of pesticides? What additional benefit does this solution have?

LEARNING STRATEGY

Personalizing: Discussing your opinion with others will help you clarify your thoughts and having clear thoughts makes writing easier.

9. Reread the following statements Dr. Caldicott makes in the article. Do you agree or disagree with her? Explain your position.

DR. CALDICOTT'S OPINION	YOUR OPINION
1. There is no single issue that is the most pressing.	______________
2. . . .many Americans are fed up with the lack of choice the two-party system offers.	______________
3. If we really commit ourselves to the task of saving the planet, we'll easily do it in ten years.	______________
4. . . .we have to take control of our country away from those who don't give a damn about what's happening to the earth, those who only care about short term profit and loss.	______________
5. Ever since the industrial revolution, we have gradually lost touch with the soil, with plants, with nature—in effect, we've lost touch with ourselves, with our own souls.	______________

C. WRITING CONVENTIONS: A PROBLEM/SOLUTION ARTICLE

Answer these questions about the writing conventions in Dr. Caldicott's article:

1. In which paragraph or paragraphs does Dr. Caldicott present the problem?
2. What solutions does Dr. Caldicott propose? Where does she propose these solutions? Does she give specific examples of how to solve the problems?
3. Does Dr. Caldicott persuade the reader to take action? How?
4. Does Dr. Caldicott use strong language to express her true feelings about the situation? Find examples of this.

Threads

Every month, there are an average of 425 oil spills and 75 chemical spills in the Great Lakes of North America.

National Wildlife Federation (1991)

SUMMARY

- Dr. Caldicott presents the problems in the first paragraph. In a problem-solution essay, present the problem or problems early in your paper.
- Dr. Caldicott proposes three solutions, two general ones, and one specific one. The first solution is working within the political system. She discusses this in Paragraphs 3–6. She discusses the second solution, direct action, in paragraphs 7–8. She then concludes with a specific problem and a specific solution, health problems caused by environmental toxins, in Paragraphs 9–10.
- Always give concrete examples of your solution(s). Dr. Caldicott gives concrete examples for each of her solutions: For the first one, electing politicians who do not represent special-interest groups, for the second, dismantling bulldozers that are used in deforestation, and lastly growing pesticide-free fruits and vegetables for the problem of pesticide use.
- Dr. Caldicott uses cause/result statements to persuade readers to take action. In Paragraph 2, she says, ". . . if we don't start now, in ten years, it will be too late."
- Caldicott also uses strong language to motivate readers. For example, in Paragraph 6, she says, ". . . we have to take control of our country away from those who don't give a damn about what's happening to the earth . . ." In paragraph 10, she says, "We're dying, and we're killing the earth as well."
- It's a good idea to say what you truly believe; it adds strength to your writing. It actually makes your job easier if you tell the truth using language that expresses your true feelings.

PRACTICE WRITING

Use your ideas from your **Quickwrite** in Part I to write a new paragraph on one environmental problem. Include

- a statement of the problem
- at least one solution
- a concrete example of the solution
- at least one cause/result statement

If you like, include a strong, emotional statement that expresses your true feelings, as Caldicott does.

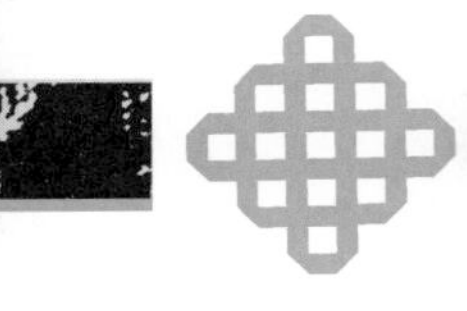

PART III

Gather Information and Propose a Solution

A. ORGANIZE AND DEVELOP YOUR IDEAS

Work in small groups. Select five environmental issues that most interest you. Do some reading on these issues. Collect specific details about the problems and possible solutions. Bring pictures that illustrate the problems and solutions, if you can. Organize your information in the following work box. You may use Dr. Caldicott's ideas and/or ideas of your own. Be prepared to explain exactly how each solution will correct the problem.

Threads

A recent survey found that one half of American farmers are concerned about using chemicals in farming.

PROBLEMS	POSSIBLE SOLUTIONS	
Problem 1:	a.	______________________
	b.	______________________
	c.	______________________
Problem 2:	a.	______________________
	b.	______________________
	c.	______________________
Problem 3:	a.	______________________
	b.	______________________
	c.	______________________
Problem 4:	a.	______________________
	b.	______________________
	c.	______________________
Problem 5:	a.	______________________
	b.	______________________
	c.	______________________

B. SHARE

Now, present your ideas to the class. Ask and answer questions about each other's solutions. Make sure you explain the solutions clearly. Give examples of how each would work.

LEARNING STRATEGY

Managing Your Learning: Organizing information before you write will help you write a well-organized essay.

C. PREPARE

On your own, select the environmental issue you feel the most strongly about and fill in the following outline.

- What is the problem?

  ____

  ____

  ____

  ____

- What are the causes and/or effects of the problem?

  ____

  ____

  ____

  ____

- What is the solution?

  ____

  ____

  ____

  ____

- What exactly should people do about this problem? How should they do it? When should they do it?, etc. (Give specific examples of how to solve the problem.)

  ____

  ____

  ____

  ____

- What will happen if people do not take action/if the problem is not solved?

  ____

  ____

  ____

  ____

Threads

1992 polls showed that people considered ozone depletion, garbage, and toxic waste the greatest environmental problems facing the U.S.

D. WRITE!

Now you are ready to write. Choose one of the following topics. As you write, keep in mind the goals you set in previous chapters.

1. Write about the environmental problem you feel the strongest about and propose one or more solution(s).

After completing assignment 1, try the following for further practice:

2. Think of a question about an environmental problem and do research to find the answer. For example: When did people first become interested in saving the planet? What are people in different parts of the world doing to save the environment? How do environmental problems in one country affect another country? Summarize the information you gather in 3-5 paragraphs.
3. Explain what you think the quote at the beginning of this chapter means. Give examples to support your explanation.

The only thing that makes civilization go forward is the responsibility of individuals . . . for the species, for the culture, for the larger thing outside ourselves.
—Wallace Stegner, American writer

4. Combine ideas from a previous chapter with ideas from this chapter. For example, write about the environmental problems of your favorite place (Chapter 5), a song that deals with the environment (Chapter 6), a movie about an environmental problem (Chapter 8), or about the environmental consequences of technological innovations (Chapter 9).

Assess

A. REFLECT

On the Reflections on My Writing chart (see Appendix A), fill in the boxes for Chapter 10: Saving the Planet.

Threads

More U.S. citizens say they are conserving energy to help the environment.

B. EXCHANGE

Exchange your paper with a classmate and answer these questions:

1. Does your partner state the problem early in the paper?
2. Are there concrete examples of the solution or solutions?
3. Does your partner make you want to take action? How? (What kind of language persuades you?)

C. REWRITE

Rewrite your paper, or just the parts that your partner or teacher found to be incomplete or unclear. As you write, consider the answers to the questions in Exercise B, or any other recommendations your partner had. Also, check to see that you have improved the area(s) you wanted to work on at the end of Chapter 9 (see Chapter 9, p. 114).

D. LOOK AHEAD

Now, write **one thing** you would like to improve the next time you write a paper.

I'm going to work on. . .

____

____

____

____

____

Appendix

APPENDIX A: REFLECTIONS ON MY WRITING

Fill in the appropriate boxes for each chapter.

CHAPTER/TOPIC	THREE THINGS I'VE LEARNED	QUESTIONS I STILL HAVE
1: Memories	__________ __________ __________	__________ __________ __________
2: Special People	__________ __________ __________	__________ __________ __________
3: Names	__________ __________ __________	__________ __________ __________
4: Learning Styles	__________ __________ __________	__________ __________ __________
5: Places	__________ __________ __________	__________ __________ __________
6: Music as Personal History	__________ __________ __________	__________ __________ __________
7: Celebrations	__________ __________ __________	__________ __________ __________
8: Movies	__________ __________ __________	__________ __________ __________
9: Future Gadgets	__________ __________ __________	__________ __________ __________
10: Saving the Planet	__________ __________ __________	__________ __________ __________

APPENDIX B: WORD LISTS

Use these word lists for further practice and review.

MEMORIES

detail
event
incident
(of something)
journal (entry)
the past
scary, scared
unforgettable

dramatic
embarrassing, embarrassed
frightening, frightened

memorable

to recall
to remember
to remind someone

SPECIAL PEOPLE

characteristic
personal quality
relative

to admire
to care about
to look up to
to respect

PHYSICAL CHARACTERISTICS

attractive
fat
good-looking
heavy
muscular

petite
plain
short
skinny

stocky
strong
tall
thin

PERSONALITY CHARACTERISTICS

cheerful
friendly
happy
open

quiet
reserved
shy
warm

NAMES

custom
honor
namesake
tradition

common
traditional
unusual

to be named after
to be named by
to be named for
to honor

LEARNING STYLES

mode
strategies
task

analytic
auditory
competitive
cooperative
kinesthetic
relational
visual

to memorize

PLACES

cluttered
crowded
dark
modern
noisy
old fashioned
quiet

airy
clean
peace, peaceful
light
peace, peaceful
spacious

to get peace and quiet
to spend time

POPULAR MUSIC

ballad
beat
drum
flute
guitar
hillbilly
idol
instruments
jazz
lyrics
orchestra
piano
pop
reggae
rhythm and blues
rock
tune

classical
romantic

to popularize

CELEBRATIONS

ball
celebration
costume
evil spirits
feast
mask
period of, time of
rite of passage
symbol

elaborate
traditional

to bring luck
to dress up
to insure
to play tricks

traditionally

MOVIES

actor, actress
cinematography
classic movie
dialogue
director
location
movie still
performance
scene
script
special effects
theme music
(the amount or type of) violence

to act

to direct

FUTURE GADGETS

gadget
innovation
invention
process
product
research, researcher
technology

complex
innovative
simple
technological

to come up with
to develop
to invent
to operate
to simplify
to work

on the market

SAVING THE PLANET

activism
deforestation
(to take) direct action
extinction
issue
ozone depletion
pesticides
short term profit
species
toxins

endangered
obsolete

to accomplish
to commit (oneself) to
to engage in

APPENDIX C: FLUENCY STARTERS

Use these sentence starters to increase your writing fluency on the following topics. Choose one or more of these starters to get your ideas flowing. Don't worry about grammar or spelling. Write as much as you can.

CHAPTER/TOPIC	FLUENCY STARTERS
1. Memories	I'll never forget. . . I have always wanted to forget. . . My memory is best when. . .
2. A person You Admire	What I admire most about him/her is. . . I never thought I would admire this person today. .. She or he influenced me because. . .
3. Names	The most ridiculous name I heard was. . . I love this name because. . . Names are meaningful because. . .
4. Learning Styles	I was always good at. . . I could never. . . I have taught myself. . .
5. Places	I am afraid when I go. . . I love to be. . . My special place is. . .
6. Music	I used to listen to. . . I really hate. . . My friends and I. . .
7. Celebrations	The party I will never forget was. . . To me, celebrations are. . . My favorite part of celebrations is. . .
8. Movies	I've recently seen. . . I prefer to watch. . . American movies are. . .
9. Gadgets	My favorite personal gadget is. . . What I need is. . . I predict we will have. . .
10. Saving the Planet	The biggest problem we have is. . . I want to. . . We must all. . .